THE
ENGLISH
GRAMMAR
WORKBOOK
FOR GRADES 3, 4, AND 5

THE ENGLISH GRAMMAR WORKBOOK FOR GRADES 3, 4, AND 5

140+ Simple Exercises to Improve Grammar, Punctuation, and Word Usage

SHELLY REES

callisto
publishing
an imprint of Sourcebooks

Published by Callisto Publishing LLC C/O Sourcebooks LLC
P.O. Box 4410, Naperville, Illinois 60567-4410
(630) 961-3900
callistopublishing.com

This product conforms to all applicable CPSC and CPSIA standards.

Source of Production: Wing King Tong Paper Products Co.Ltd. Shenzhen, Guangdong Province, China
Date of Production: January 2024
Run Number: 5037729

Printed and bound in China
WKT 2

To my mom, for her sharing of the blue book, and to my husband, Aric, for his unwavering support and encouragement.

CONTENTS

INTRODUCTION

Let's face it: Grammar is not everyone's favorite topic. Understanding the rules of grammar can feel like an arduous and challenging task. Many teachers find teaching grammar to be one of the dullest parts of their jobs.

This book can change all of that. With interesting, engaging lessons and practice activities all laid out in an easy-to-follow format, students will begin to look forward to grammar lessons. Teachers and parents who struggle with topics like parts of speech, capitalization, and punctuation will find this book to be a path to better grammar instruction.

As a student, I actually loved grammar. The certainty of rules and structure appealed to me. I had a wonderful teacher who showed me the joy of diagramming sentences—yes, joy and grammar can coexist!

Later, as an elementary school teacher, I shared my love of grammar with my own students. I created fun games and activities for them to use so that they could better understand normally confusing concepts. They responded with improved skills and confidence in their daily speech and writing.

Many teachers I worked with knew of my love of writing and grammar. They often came to me for proofreading and editing help. When they had questions about grammar lessons they were teaching, they asked about my pedagogical methods for those topics.

This book is a way for me to help more teachers, parents, and students with their grammar struggles. I am excited to share my lessons, activities, and ideas with a larger audience.

The activities in this book will help you and your students better understand the important grammar skills they need to be better communicators through writing and speaking. I have built each lesson to be interesting and fun; the results will be worth the time investment.

HOW TO USE THIS BOOK

This book will serve as the main base for your grammar classes and lessons. I chose the topics based on decades of teaching experience and education standards. These topics are the most commonly taught grammar concepts for grades 3, 4, and 5. This book does not cover all grammar concepts, but students completing the lessons will gain a solid foundation for further lessons.

The lessons in this book move from simpler concepts to more difficult ones. Part 1 aligns with third-grade standards, Part 2 aligns with fourth-grade standards, and Part 3 aligns with fifth-grade standards. Keep in mind that, because students learn at different paces, they can move throughout the book at different speeds and sequences as needed.

The topics are divided into 60 lessons. Additionally, there are activity pages and quizzes included throughout the book.

Please note:

- Each grade level has 20 lessons.
- There are two practice exercises following each lesson.
- Each grade level includes fun activity pages based on various grammar topics.
- All answers are located at the back of the book.

Because mastery of concepts can be assessed with the completion of the practice exercises and fun pages, there are no tests found in the units.

I have included everything you and your students need in order to become more successful with grammar. By mastering these fundamental concepts of language and grammar, students will become better communicators in both spoken and written language.

PART 1

GRADE 3

SUBJECTS AND PREDICATES

The **complete subject** is all the words in the subject part of a sentence. It names someone or something and tells who or what the sentence is about.

The **complete predicate** is all the words in the predicate part of a sentence. The predicate part tells what the subject is or does.

Every sentence gives a complete thought. In order to do that, **the sentence has to have two main parts**. The **subject** part names someone or something. The **predicate** part tells what the subject is or does.

Read the following sentences. The part in blue is the complete subject. The part in green is the complete predicate.

Many different sports **are played during the summer.**

Soccer **is a very popular sport.**

Our best hitter **has broken his wrist.**

A swim on a hot day **can cool you down.**

Both complete subjects and complete predicates may have just one word or more than one word.

Here are some examples of sentences with just one word in both the subjects and predicates, divided by a | :

Horses | gallop.

Boats | float.

Carpenters | build.

By adding more descriptive words and specific information, the subjects and predicates can become longer:

The beautiful horses | gallop across the field.

Many different boats | float on the lake.

Hard-working carpenters | build houses and buildings.

PRACTICE EXERCISE 1.1

Directions: Write a | between the complete subject and the complete predicate.
Example: Her sprained ankle | began to swell.

1. Two friends went to the restaurant together.

2. Our science teacher pointed to a model of a skeleton.

3. His hobby is collecting old postage stamps.

4. Gabe's horse pushed open the gate with its nose.

5. Mrs. Wright bought a new pair of glasses.

PRACTICE EXERCISE 1.2

Directions: Underline the complete subject once and the complete predicate twice.
Example: A chameleon blends in with the colors around it.

1. The soccer team practiced the new play for an hour.

2. The teacher wrote a quick e-mail to the parents.

3. The pitcher was filled with freshly squeezed orange juice.

4. Izzy ate a piece of chocolate cake for dessert.

5. A cactus survives with very little water.

6. A warm sweater feels so nice on a chilly day.

7. The group of deer ran into the woods.

8. A pesky mosquito keeps buzzing in my ear.

NOUNS

A **noun** is a word that names a person, place, thing, or idea.

Without nouns, it would be very difficult to speak or write about specific things. Nouns are words that name people, places, things, and even ideas.

EXAMPLES OF NOUNS			
People	**Places**	**Things**	**Ideas**
man	school	baseball	bravery
child	country	tablet	humor
aunt	Ohio	desk	courage
Lisa	beach	cereal	love
teacher	Main Street	bicycle	suggestion
baker	Atlantic Ocean	Snickers	wealth

PRACTICE EXERCISE 2.1

Directions: There are three nouns in each sentence. Underline each noun.
Example: The <u>dogs</u> howled and barked as the <u>cars</u> and <u>trucks</u> drove by.

1. The family was excited to be driving the new car to the beach.

2. Mr. Lee had packed sandwiches into a blue cooler.

3. The children laughed as they jumped into the sand and ran toward the ocean.

4. Ms. Lee helped set up an umbrella and beach chairs.

5. Jenny's oldest brother took his surfboard and rode into the waves.

PRACTICE EXERCISE 2.2

Directions: Underline the nouns in each sentence.
Example: My <u>grandma</u> placed the <u>turkey</u>, <u>potatoes</u>, and <u>carrots</u> on the <u>table</u>.

1. The team gathered before the game to make a plan.

2. The crowd cheered as the first pitch was thrown.

3. As the pitcher threw the ball, the batter waited nervously.

4. He swung his bat, and the baseball flew to the outfield.

5. At the concession stand, fans were buying popcorn and peanuts.

6. The sun beat down, and the players became extremely hot.

7. The people were grateful when a soft breeze entered the stadium.

CONCRETE AND ABSTRACT NOUNS

An **abstract noun** is a word that is an idea, quality, concept, or event. It is not **concrete**, meaning you cannot touch, feel, or see it.

Many nouns are concrete. You can see, feel, touch, or even smell or taste them.

For example, these are **concrete nouns**:

cupcake   tomato   house   cloud   automobile   phone   lawn

Other nouns are abstract. You cannot see, feel, touch, smell, or taste them. Instead, they are ideas, qualities, or events.

For example, these are **abstract nouns**:

joy   wealth   anger   confusion   luxury   sorrow   happiness

| EXAMPLES OF CONCRETE AND ABSTRACT NOUNS ||
Concrete Nouns	Abstract Nouns
sister	wisdom
church	horror
carpet	kindness
dishes	dream
teacher	goal
lake	friendship
avenue	success
pie	dishonesty

PRACTICE EXERCISE 3.1

Directions: Note whether each word is a concrete or an abstract noun.
Example: happiness <u>abstract</u>

1. couch _____

2. peace _____

3. courage _____

4. pumpkin _____

5. wealth _____

PRACTICE EXERCISE 3.2

Directions: Underline the concrete nouns once and underline the abstract nouns twice.
Example: My <u>teacher</u> read a <u>book</u> about <u>freedom</u> to the <u>class</u>.

1. What is the lesson we are learning today in school?

2. The immigrants showed great courage in moving to a new country.

3. The pioneers often faced hardships and felt sorrow as they crossed the prairie.

4. Did you share your dream of success with your parents?

5. If you think your invention will help people, you should make it.

6. The pizza was baking in the oven, and my hunger grew.

7. As we drove to the beach in the car, our boredom turned into excitement.

8. How much candy do you think we will get at the parade?

COMMON AND PROPER NOUNS

A **common noun** is the general name of any person place, thing, or idea.

A **proper noun** names a specific person, place, thing, or idea.

Some nouns are capitalized, while others are not. Nouns that are not capitalized (unless they are the first word in a sentence) are called **common nouns**. They name any person, place, thing, or idea. They aren't specific.

The common nouns are italicized in this sentence:

Jeffrey climbed into the *seat* of the *roller coaster*.

Nouns that are capitalized are called **proper nouns**. They name a specific person, place, thing, or idea. For example, while *boy* is a common noun, *Daniel* is a proper noun. *Daniel* is the name of a specific boy.

The proper nouns are italicized in this sentence:

Jeffrey climbed into the seat of the *Dragon Coaster*.

EXAMPLES OF COMMON AND PROPER NOUNS	
Common Nouns	**Proper Nouns**
city	Denver
lake	Lake Tahoe
person	Christina
amusement park	Disneyland
street	Main Street

Some proper nouns may be more than one word. For example, *Oak Street, Yellowstone National Park,* and *Aunt Jenny* are all proper nouns that include more than one word. Be sure to capitalize each word of the proper noun.

PRACTICE EXERCISE 4.1

Directions: Write whether the underlined noun is a common or proper noun.

Example: Many people crowded into the <u>elevator</u>. common noun

1. Joshua read a biography of <u>Abraham Lincoln</u>. _____

2. The family went out for <u>dinner</u> last Friday. _____

3. Uncle Troy fished in <u>Pine Creek</u> for some trout. _____

4. She hopes to visit <u>Florida</u> on her next vacation. _____

5. <u>Girls</u> carrying umbrellas stepped onto the sidewalk. _____

PRACTICE EXERCISE 4.2

Directions: Underline the common nouns once and the proper nouns twice.

Example: <u>Grant</u> rode the <u>bus</u> from <u>Houston</u> to <u>Dallas</u>.

1. A sunset over Lake Erie is a beautiful sight.

2. The musician played Sonata Number 5 as people strolled by.

3. Terrence and Joel talked as they walked down Sackett Avenue.

4. We had a wonderful view from our seats at the Sunset Steakhouse.

5. My mother ordered steak, shrimp, and rolls for her meal.

6. Aunt Pauline wanted to buy us all some dessert at the Hawaiian Ice Shack.

7. Later that night, the family went to the house to play Monopoly.

8. Weston planned on buying all four railroads and Park Place on the board.

CAPITALIZATION OF PROPER NOUNS

A proper noun begins with a capital letter.

A proper noun always begins with a capital letter. If the noun has more than one word, each important word in the noun is capitalized.

Examples: Colorado, James, Main Street, and the Statue of Liberty

This chart gives some rules and examples for capitalizing proper nouns.

CAPITALIZING PROPER NOUNS		
Rule	**Examples**	
Capitalize the names of people and pets.	Jamie Mrs. Wright Lassie	Marshall Americans
Capitalize the names of months, days, and holidays.	May October Tuesday	Saturday Fourth of July Thanksgiving
Capitalize every important word in the names of specific places and things.	United States Rocky Mountains Wyoming Golden Gate Bridge	New York City Liberty Bell South America

PRACTICE EXERCISE 5.1

Directions: Underline the words in each list that should be capitalized.
Example: city, girl, <u>joe</u>, <u>park hotel</u>, street, <u>florida</u>

1. harriet, flew, week, georgia, the

2. everglades national park, alligator, sights, disneyland, zoo

3. friday, drive, gulf of mexico, brought, ocean

4. third street, family, orlando, boston, airport

5. airplane, vacation, smith, leah, sequoia national park

PRACTICE EXERCISE 5.2

Directions: Underline the words in each sentence that should be capitalized.
Example: The bridge crosses over the <u>mississippi river</u>.

1. many movies are made in hollywood.

2. the jones family traveled to california in june.

3. they visited disneyland and saw the pacific ocean.

4. mary and jenna had never been to the beach before.

5. on thursday, the family walked down hollywood boulevard.

6. they ate at the celebrity café and saw several famous people.

7. on saturday, they saw the golden gate bridge in san francisco.

8. before they came home, they visited muir woods national monument and saw mount whitney.

SINGULAR AND PLURAL NOUNS

A **singular noun** names one person, place, thing, or idea.

A **plural noun** names more than one person, place, thing, or idea.

Nouns can name just one thing (singular) or more than one thing (plural).

The **singular nouns** are italicized in this sentence:

My *mother* bought new lamps for the *living room*.

The **plural nouns** are italicized in this sentence:

The *campers* brought a tent, *lanterns*, and *lunches*.

Often, the plural form of a noun is made by adding an *-s* or *-es* to the end of the singular noun. Other times, the plural form is made in other ways, depending upon the ending of the singular noun or the noun itself.

RULES FOR FORMING PLURAL NOUNS		
Rule		**Examples**
most nouns	add -s	cat → cats
nouns that end in *s*, *sh*, *x*, *ch*, or *z*	add -es; for words ending in *z*, add an extra *z* before the -es	brush → brushes quiz → quizzes fox → foxes
nouns ending in *f* or *fe*	sometimes, change the *f* to *v* and add -es	wife → wives shelf → shelves
nouns ending in a consonant and *y*	change the *y* to *i* and add -es	city → cities puppy → puppies
nouns ending in *o*	add -es	potato → potatoes

RULES FOR FORMING PLURAL NOUNS		
	Rule	Examples
various nouns	don't add or change anything	deer → deer sheep → sheep
irregular nouns	no specific rule	child → children man → men

PRACTICE EXERCISE 6.1

Directions: Underline the noun in each list of words. Then note whether it is singular or plural.
Example: bake, cookies, listens, sweet, delicious plural

1. paper, raps, ended _____

2. talking, smiled, playgrounds _____

3. bought, an, beanbag, the _____

PRACTICE EXERCISE 6.2

Directions: Write the plural form of each singular noun.
Example: garage garages

1. bat _____

2. village _____

3. glass _____

4. turkey _____

5. flag _____

6. box _____

WHAT IS A NOUN?

Name _____ Date _____

Directions: Color all the gumballs in each row that are nouns.

Row 1: noun — zipper, travel, listen, Main Street, planet, pretty, Texas

Row 2: noun — curious, Harry Potter, shout, joy, First Central Bank, funny, giraffe

Row 3: noun — cousin, bridge, swim, famous, Dr. Mix, catcher, bright

Row 4: noun — office, carry, Disney World, sunlight, Leah, over, jealous

Row 5: noun — broken, books, Emma, quick, peace, Europe, trail

14

COMMON NOUNS

Name _____ Date _____

Directions: It's time to **Roll and Mark** the common nouns. First, roll one die. Find the number you rolled on the chart. Then complete that action for all the common nouns in the first sentence. Repeat the process and work your way through the rest of the sentences.

Number Rolled	Action	Number Rolled	Action
1	Circle all common nouns.	4	Underline the common nouns with a wavy line.
2	Underline all common nouns.	5	Draw a box around the common nouns.
3	Highlight all common nouns.	6	Choose any action from 1–5.

	Number Rolled	Sentences
1)		The tiny kitten shivered as it say by the open window.
2)		The students painted posters to hang on the wall in the hallway.
3)		The two friends put their backpacks and coats in their lockers.
4)		The traveler carried a suitcase through Denver Airport.
5)		The commercial compares two brands of oatmeal.
6)		The family planted corn, beans, tomatoes, and lettuce in the garden.
7)		The runners laced up their sneakers and stretched their legs.
8)		His sister finished the puzzle and decided to bake some cookies.
9)		The parade will start at noon on the street in front of City Hall.
10)		George did not want to do his homework, so he read a book instead.

IRREGULAR PLURAL NOUNS

An **irregular plural noun** is a noun that does not become plural by adding -*s* or -*es*. Instead, the word is made plural by changing vowels, changing the word, or adding a different ending.

Most plural nouns are regular, meaning you simply add an -*s* or an -*es* to the singular noun to make it plural. Irregular plural nouns don't always follow simple rules.

For example, these are regular plural nouns:

cookies   tables   computers   oceans   pizzas

These are irregular plural nouns:

children   deer   feet   loaves   men   oxen

If the singular noun ends in *f*, the plural is formed by changing the *f* to *v* and adding -*es*. For example, *wolf* becomes *wolves*.

Other irregular nouns can be formed by changing vowels or changing the word itself. For example, *goose* becomes *geese* and *child* becomes *children*.

EXAMPLES OF IRREGULAR PLURAL NOUNS			
Singular Nouns		**Plural Nouns**	
elf	man	elves	men
knife	mouse	knives	mice
shelf	child	shelves	children
loaf	foot	loaves	feet
calf	goose	calves	geese

PRACTICE EXERCISE 7.1

Directions: There is a misspelled irregular plural noun in each sentence. Underline it and then spell it correctly on the line.
Example: The <u>elfs</u> worked together to fix the shoes. <u>elves</u>

1. Jaelle lost two tooths in the same day. _____

2. How many gooses did you see at the lake? _____

3. There were several childs playing at the park. _____

4. The oxes were pulling the cart across the field. _____

5. Please buy three loafs of bread at the store. _____

PRACTICE EXERCISE 7.2

Directions: Write the plural form of each singular noun.
Example: ax <u>axes</u>

1. scarf _____

2. thief _____

3. woman _____

4. wife _____

5. die _____

6. foot _____

7. crisis _____

8. mouse _____

9. man _____

10. louse _____

11. quiz _____

12. ox _____

13. self _____

14. wolf _____

15. goose _____

POSSESSIVES

A **possessive** is a word that shows ownership. It shows that someone or something owns something else.

Remember that a noun names a person, place, thing, or idea. When a noun owns another thing, it is possessive.

The **possessive nouns** are italicized in each of the following sentences:

1. *Miranda's* grandfather came to visit.
2. The *dog's* tail wagged.
3. Those *flowers'* petals are a pretty yellow color.

In sentence 1, the grandfather belongs to Miranda.
In sentence 2, the tail belongs to the dog.
In sentence 3, the petals belong to the flowers.
When writing a possessive noun, you have to decide where to place the apostrophe ('). Use these rules to help you.

MAKING POSSESSIVE NOUNS		
To make the possessive of	**Add**	**Example**
a singular noun	's	cat's tail, James's shirt, niece's wallet, lion's mane
a plural noun ending in *s*	,	hens' eggs, neighbors' houses, cousins' voices
a plural noun not ending in *s*	's	women's jobs, children's books, men's cars

Examples:

Tablets that belong to Sheila → Sheila's tablets

Hats that belong to kids → kids' hats

Tails that belong to mice → mice's tails

PRACTICE EXERCISE 8.1

Directions: Underline each possessive noun.
Example: <u>Cora's</u> house is next door.

1. That car's tire was flat.

2. The teachers' meeting lasts an hour.

3. The children's singing filled the room.

4. I borrowed Kelly's bicycle.

5. The artists' paintbrushes are new.

PRACTICE EXERCISE 8.2

Directions: Write the possessive form of each noun.
Example: flower <u>flower's</u>

1. officers _____

2. men _____

3. hotel _____

4. neighbors _____

5. coaches _____

6. actors _____

7. leader _____

8. Mr. Rich _____

9. mouse _____

10. workers _____

ACTION VERBS

An **action verb** is a word that shows action.

An action verb tells what the subject of the sentence does. It explains what a noun is doing, has done, or will do.

For example, these are **action verbs**:

run   hide   discuss   learn   eat   laugh   howl

An action verb expresses something that a person, animal, or object can do. To decide if a word is an action verb, look at the sentence and ask yourself if the word shows that someone is doing something. If it is, then it is an action verb.

Read this sentence:

The cat *purrs* loudly.

Since the word *purrs* shows that the cat is doing something, it is an action verb.

Keep in mind that there can be more than one action verb in a sentence.

The italicized words in the following sentences are some examples of action verbs in sentences:

Kayla *reached* the finish line first.

The noodles *boiled* over the top of the cooking pan.

The deer *jumped* over the fence and *ran* out of sight.

Think about some things you are good at doing. Do you *read* well? Are you able to *run* quickly? Do you *listen* patiently to your friends? Make a list of those action words.

PRACTICE EXERCISE 9.1

Directions: Look at each group of words. Underline the action verbs in each list.
Example: shoes, <u>walk</u>, boots, sandals, <u>run</u>

1. dog, bark, collar, jump, howl

2. play, guitar, instrument, lesson, strum

3. cake, bake, cookies, mix, stir

4. swim, pool, dive, splash, water

5. road, drive, ride, highway, car

PRACTICE EXERCISE 9.2

Directions: Underline the action verb(s) in each sentence.
Example: Our family always <u>eats</u> dinner at five o'clock.

1. My friend invited twenty people to the party.

2. The hikers carried their supplies in their backpacks.

3. The kitten meowed and jumped across the floor.

4. The students choose a leader each day.

5. My father paints murals for the city.

6. We told the teacher about the broken door.

7. Keisha laughed and cried with happiness when she won the contest.

8. The doctor removed the cast from Eric's arm.

VERB TENSE

The **tense** of a **verb** shows the time when an action takes place.

There are three main tenses of verbs: past, present, and future.

Verbs in the **past tense** describe an action that already happened. The past tense is usually formed by adding -*ed* to the verb.

Example: The students *studied* for the test.

Verbs in the **present tense** describe an action that is happening right now.

Example: The students *study* for the test.

Verbs in the **future tense** describe an action that will happen. The future tense is usually formed by adding the words *will* or *shall* before the verb.

The students *will study* for the test.

Here are some examples of verbs in each of the three tenses.

VERB TENSE		
Past Tense	**Present Tense**	**Future Tense**
hurried	hurry	will hurry
scared	scare	will scare
answered	answer	will answer
heard	hear	will hear
spied	spy	will spy

Some verbs are irregular and don't follow the normal rules for forming the past tense.

For example, the past tense of *fall* is *fell* and the past tense of *ride* is *rode*.

PRACTICE EXERCISE 10.1

Directions: Underline the verb in each sentence. Then write *past tense, present tense,* or *future tense* on the line to show which tense it is.
Example: We <u>saved</u> two dollars during the sale. <u>past tense</u>

1. The cast will perform the play at 8:00 tonight. _____

2. My brother answered my mother's questions. _____

3. The bride threw the bouquet of flowers. _____

4. This cake tastes delicious! _____

5. The teacher will help her students tomorrow. _____

PRACTICE EXERCISE 10.2

Directions: Complete the table by writing the verbs in the missing tenses. The first row is filled out as an example.

VERB TENSE		
Past Tense	**Present Tense**	**Future Tense**
asked	ask	will ask
used		
	need	
		will practice
	slam	
typed		
arrived		

IRREGULAR VERBS

Irregular verbs don't form the past tense by adding -*ed*.

The past tense of most verbs is made by adding -*ed* to the end of the word. Irregular verbs do not follow this rule.

The past tense forms of some common irregular verbs are shown in the following chart. The **past participle** is the verb form used with the helping verbs *has, had,* or *have*.

COMMON IRREGULAR VERBS		
Present	**Past**	**Past Participle**
break	broke	has broken
come	came	has come
do	did	has done
eat	ate	has eaten
fall	fell	has fallen
fly	flew	has flown
freeze	froze	has frozen
give	gave	has given
go	went	has gone
grow	grew	has grown

Be careful that you don't just add -*ed* to the end of an irregular verb to make the past tense.

For example, you wouldn't say, "I *growed* two inches last year."

Instead, you would say, "I *grew* two inches last year."

PRACTICE EXERCISE 11.1

Directions: Write the correct past tense of each verb.
Example: take: <u>took</u>

1. see: _____

2. do: _____

3. write: _____

4. eat: _____

5. give: _____

PRACTICE EXERCISE 11.2

Directions: Complete the table by writing the irregular verbs in the past tense. The first row is filled in as an example for you.

PAST TENSE OF IRREGULAR VERBS	
Present Tense	**Past Tense**
bring	brought
think	
swim	
freeze	
ride	
fall	
write	
go	

PRONOUNS

A **pronoun** is a word that takes the place of a noun.

In the first sentence of each of the following pairs of sentences, the words in blue are nouns. In the second sentence, the words in green are pronouns taking the place of the nouns.

1.   **Lisa** has curly hair. **She** has curly hair.
2.   Paul invited **Lauren** and **Aaron**. Paul invited **them**.

In sentence 1, the word *she* takes the place of *Lisa.*
In sentence 2, the word *them* takes the place of *Lauren* and *Aaron.*
Singular pronouns refer to just one person, place, or thing.
Plural pronouns refer to more than one person, place, or thing.
This chart shows the singular and plural pronouns.

PRONOUNS	
Singular Pronouns	**Plural Pronouns**
I, me, my, mine	we, us, our, ours
you, your, yours	you, your, yours
she, he, it, her, him, hers, his, its	they, them, their, theirs

A **possessive pronoun** shows that something belongs to someone or something.

If the tablet belongs to me, it is *my* tablet. It is *mine.*

If the bike belongs to you, it is *your* bike. It is *yours.*

If the cupcake belongs to her, it is *her* cupcake. It is *hers.*

Other possessive pronouns include *his, its, our, ours, your, yours, their,* and *theirs.*

PRACTICE EXERCISE 12.1

Directions: Underline the pronoun in each sentence.
Example: Is this book <u>mine</u>?

1. I cannot wait to have some pizza for dinner!

2. Would you rather have cookies or ice cream for dessert?

3. Which movie is she going to watch tonight?

4. We were excited to roast marshmallows over the campfire.

5. Ms. Shear told us some surprising news.

PRACTICE EXERCISE 12.2

Directions: Read the first sentence. Replace the underlined word in each sentence with a pronoun in the second sentence.
Example: <u>The students</u> carried the books. <u>They</u> carried the books.

1. The piano is <u>Jim's</u>. The piano is _____.

2. <u>Barrett and Bailey</u> are twins. _____ are twins.

3. <u>Diana's</u> set of markers is brand-new.
   _____ set of markers is brand-new.

4. <u>Alisha</u> decided to make a movie.
   _____ decided to make a movie.

5. Sam asked <u>Michael</u> to help bake pies.
   Sam asked _____ to help bake pies.

6. Give the pencils to <u>Rita and me</u>, please.
   Give the pencils to _____, please.

ABSTRACT NOUNS

Name _____ Date _____

Directions: Find and circle or highlight each abstract noun in the word search.
Words can be found across, backward, up and down, or diagonal.

BRAVERY	SUCCESS	TRUST	ANGER
SKILL	COURAGE	DEDICATION	PEACE
MISERY	BELIEF	FRIENDSHIP	PAIN
HONESTY	LIBERTY	PROGRESS	THOUGHT
LOYALTY	KNOWLEDGE	LOVE	CULTURE

```
S  D  E  D  I  C  A  T  I  O  N  L  O  Y  B  T
M  A  U  V  S  C  E  G  A  R  U  O  C  H  R  S
L  I  P  R  O  G  R  E  S  S  S  D  F  B  A  E
I  P  S  T  G  L  K  S  A  P  S  E  R  H  V  G
B  A  M  E  R  K  N  U  I  A  E  D  I  G  E  D
E  I  I  T  R  U  O  H  F  I  C  I  G  U  R  E
R  C  S  R  S  Y  S  A  R  N  C  F  R  O  Y  L
T  U  E  O  T  D  W  T  H  O  U  G  H  T  V  W
Y  L  P  V  N  R  P  R  O  G  S  M  I  S  E  O
B  T  B  E  L  I  E  F  A  N  G  K  R  Y  B  N
E  U  I  T  A  N  G  E  R  E  R  F  I  K  R  K
L  R  S  H  O  C  A  Y  T  L  A  Y  O  L  T  H
F  E  K  Y  T  S  E  N  O  H  U  G  H  T  L  Y
```

ACTION VERBS

Name _____ Date _____

Directions: Color all the baseballs in each row that are action verbs.

action verb — teacher — listen — lake — discuss — climb — short — tennis

action verb — help — pitcher — catch — lazy — sing — read — soda

action verb — near — inspire — imagine — explore — see — door — next

action verb — goes — zipper — swims — letter — aunt — ask — couch

action verb — throw — wrist — win — travel — pretty — painful — write

ADJECTIVES

An **adjective** is a word that describes a noun or pronoun.

An adjective tells something about a noun. It can tell how many or what kind.

Read the following paragraph. Some of the adjectives are shown in green, some are shown in blue, and some are underlined.

The Statue of Liberty is a **beautiful** statue on Liberty Island in the New York Harbor. It was a **valuable** gift from France. It has become one of the most **famous** sights in the United States. The **tall**, **copper** statue stands at a height of **305** feet. There are **354** steps leading to the **magnificent** crown inside the **amazing** statue. The **large** crown has **seven** rays, which symbolize the **seven** continents of the world. **Many** people visit the statue **each** year.

The words shown in green tell **what kind**. For example, *beautiful* describes the word *statue*, and *valuable* describes the word *gift*.

The words shown in blue tell **how many**. For example, *seven* describes the noun *rays*, and *many* describes the noun *people*.

The words that are underlined are **articles**. There are three articles: *a, an,* and *the*.

Adjectives help add description to sentences. Take the following two sentences, for example:

A cow wandered in the field.

A lonely, brown cow wandered in the wide, green field.

Doesn't the second sentence give you a much clearer picture in your mind?

As you write sentences, try to add adjectives to put a clearer picture in your readers' minds.

PRACTICE EXERCISE 13.1

Directions: Underline the adjectives (including articles) in each list of words.
Example: <u>beautiful</u>, city, <u>old</u>, <u>the</u>, listen

1. summer, exciting, is, perform, large

2. months, popular, fun, the, play

3. story, strange, words, a, tell

4. island, called, few, before, three

5. some, draw, colorful, laugh, an

PRACTICE EXERCISE 13.2

Directions: Underline the adjectives (including articles) in each sentence.
Example: <u>The</u> <u>tired</u> skier drank <u>several</u> cups of <u>hot</u> cocoa.

1. He lost two hats at the old ski lodge.

2. Jim lives on a busy street near several stores.

3. I chipped a front tooth when I bit into a hard apple.

4. Darrel read fifty pages of his new book.

5. We visited an amusement park so we could ride the exciting roller coasters.

6. Many wild geese flew over the icy, frozen lake.

7. My tired mother read three e-mails before she went to bed.

8. The large group of friends laughed as they watched the funny movie.

ADJECTIVES THAT COMPARE

Sometimes an adjective can be used to compare two or more things.

Use the **-er form** of an adjective to compare two nouns.

Use the **-est form** of an adjective to compare three or more nouns.

Adjectives describe nouns. One way they can describe is by comparing persons, places, or things.

When two nouns are being compared, use the -er form of the adjective.

For example, in the following sentence, two roller coasters are being compared:

One roller coaster is <u>faster</u> than the other.

When three or more nouns are being compared, use the -est form of the adjective. In the following example, one roller coaster is being compared with all the roller coasters in a group:

This roller coaster is the <u>fastest</u> of all.

Following are some examples of adjectives that compare.

ADJECTIVES THAT COMPARE		
Adjective	**Compares Two Nouns**	**Compares Three or More Nouns**
brave	braver	bravest
small	smaller	smallest
tall	taller	tallest
early	earlier	earliest
flat	flatter	flattest

Sometimes, you must change the spelling of a word when adding the suffixes *er* and *est*.

•	Drop final *e*:	brave	braver	bravest
•	Change final *y* to *i*:	early	earlier	earliest
•	Double final consonant:	wet	wetter	wettest

PRACTICE EXERCISE 14.1

Directions: Write the *-er* and *-est* forms of each adjective.
Example: long: <u>longer</u>, <u>longest</u>

1. sweet: _____ , _____

2. warm: _____ , _____

3. nice: _____ , _____

4. funny: _____ , _____

PRACTICE EXERCISE 14.2

Directions: Underline the word in parentheses that correctly completes each sentence.
Example: Spring is the (rainier, <u>rainiest</u>) season of all.

1. This hat is (warmer, warmest) than that one.

2. Alisha is the (faster, fastest) runner on the team.

3. Oak Avenue is the (narrower, narrowest) street in town.

4. Eli's garden is (greener, greenest) than Jessie's garden.

ADVERBS

An **adverb** is a word that describes a verb.

Adverbs answer possible questions about the action in a sentence, such as:

How?   Where?   When?   How much?   How often?

In the following examples, the verb in each sentence is underlined once. The adverb that describes the verb is underlined twice. The question the adverb answers is in parentheses:

She <u>always</u> <u>wears</u> a gold necklace. (How often does she wear it?)

<u>Yesterday</u> I <u>went</u> to the store. (When did I go to the store?)

We <u>carefully</u> <u>climbed</u> the ladder. (How did we climb the ladder?)

Following are examples of adverbs and the kind of question each generally answers.

ADVERBS				
How?	**Where?**	**When?**	**How much?**	**How often?**
slowly	nearby	today	barely	always
well	here	often	extremely	rarely
fast	there	lately	deeply	never
quietly	forward	usually	too	usually
gladly	inside	always	quite	frequently
easily	everywhere	yesterday	almost	often

Note that many adverbs end in -*ly*, especially adverbs that explain *how* an action happens.

PRACTICE EXERCISE 15.1

Directions: Underline the adverb once. Underline the verb it describes twice.
Example: My brother <u>held</u> my hand <u>tightly</u>.

1. My father mows the lawn often.

2. The baby laughed happily.

3. Tomorrow we will go to the waterpark.

4. There is a library nearby.

5. My school is getting a new playground soon.

PRACTICE EXERCISE 15.2

Directions: Underline the adverb in each sentence. Then write which kind of question the adverb answers: *How? Where? When? How much?* or *How often?*
Example: <u>Once</u> I tried to ski at Park City. <u>How often?</u>

1. Lisa often swam at the city pool. _____

2. Mr. Paulo washed the dishes carefully. _____

3. Danny watched the game quietly from the bleachers. _____

4. He leaned forward when he heard the crack of the bat. _____

5. Hours of practice helped her to play the piano well. _____

6. He usually reads a book at home. _____

7. She sometimes wins prizes when playing games. _____

8. They politely clapped for the winner. _____

CONJUNCTIONS

A **conjunction** is a word that joins together other words, phrases, or parts of sentences.

The three most-used conjunctions are *and, or,* and *but.*

Conjunctions have three main jobs:

They join words together.

Example: Would you like cookies *and* ice cream for dessert?

They join phrases together.

Example: Do you want to ride the roller coaster *or* the Tilt-a-Whirl next?

They join parts of a sentence together.

Example: I tried to hurry home, *but* I wasn't fast enough to get there in time.

There are many other conjunctions you can use to combine words, phrases, or parts of sentences:

although	because	however
if	since	therefore
though	unless	when
whenever	where	while

Some conjunctions can be used in pairs:

either/or	both/and
neither/nor	whether/or

PRACTICE EXERCISE 16.1

Directions: Underline the conjunction in each sentence.
Example: Do you like hamburgers <u>or</u> hot dogs?

1. Josie and Liam baked a cake for dessert.

2. Mike wanted to play outside after school, but it was too cold.

3. I went to the beach and played in the waves all day.

4. My mom made macaroni and cheese for dinner.

5. Justice wasn't sure whether he wanted cereal or eggs for breakfast.

PRACTICE EXERCISE 16.2

Directions: Write a conjunction to complete each sentence.
Example: Tristan <u>and</u> Gabe went to the county fair.

1. Lunch was on time, _____ it didn't taste very good.

2. Do you like apples _____ bananas?

3. The bird whistled _____ chirped when it saw the squirrel in the nearby tree.

4. We will ride on the log flume _____ not on the waterslides.

5. Our family was late to the party _____ my dad got lost on the way.

6. We visited Florida _____ Georgia on our vacation.

7. You can go swimming, _____ you need to wear sunscreen.

8. Please make me a peanut-butter-_____-jelly sandwich for lunch.

SIMPLE AND COMPOUND SENTENCES

A **simple sentence** expresses one complete thought.

A **compound sentence** uses a conjunction to join two or more simple sentences together.

A **simple sentence** has one complete subject and one complete predicate.

For example: We wanted to play baseball. The rain changed our plans.

A **compound sentence** contains two or more simple sentences. The simple sentences are joined together with the conjunction *and, or,* or *but.*

For example: We wanted to play baseball, *but* the rain changed our plans.

A simple sentence can have a compound subject or a compound predicate.

Examples:

My sister and I baked cookies. (compound subject)

We baked cookies and made ice cream. (compound predicate)

When combining two simple sentences to make a compound sentence, use a comma in front of the conjunction you are using to join the sentences.

See the following chart for more examples.

COMPOUND SENTENCES			
Simple Sentence	+ Conjunction	+ Simple Sentence	= Compound Sentence
There was a sudden rainstorm.	and	A beautiful rainbow appeared.	There was a sudden rainstorm, and a beautiful rainbow appeared.
Jill might make a cake.	or	She might buy one at the store.	Jill might make a cake, or she might buy one at the store.
You can text me when you get there.	but	It would be better if you called me.	You can text me when you get there, but it would be better if you called me.

PRACTICE EXERCISE 17.1

Directions: Note whether each sentence is simple or compound.
Example: The team ran onto the field, and the people cheered. <u>compound</u>

1. My father mailed a package to my older sister. _____

2. Leah wrote a song, and she sang it at the assembly. _____

3. Many people entered the contest, but only one winner was chosen. _____

4. Jared and Ty worked together to solve the mystery. _____

PRACTICE EXERCISE 17.2

Directions: Underline the two simple sentences in each compound sentence. Place a comma before the conjunction that joins the two simple sentences.

Example: <u>She wanted to ride the waterslide</u>, but <u>she decided to ride the roller coaster first</u>.

1. Everyone is hungry but lunch isn't ready yet.

2. I would love to have some dessert but I am too full.

3. You can ride your bike to the pool or you can walk.

4. Jess may do his homework now or he may finish it after dinner.

5. The audience clapped and the band came back onto the stage.

6. Some people have straight hair and some people have curly hair.

7. Holly went to see her friend but she was not home.

8. Many of my friends like funny books but I like mysteries.

VERB TENSE

Name _____ Date _____

Directions: Color each star as follows:

Past Tense = Red; Present Tense = Yellow; Future Tense = Blue

went

rang

mention

wrote

wander

warned

will find

grew

appear

will travel

will eat

choose

opened

warns

needed

will ask

sail

41

CAPITALIZATION IN TITLES

Capitalize the first word, the last word, and all important words in the title of a book. Book titles are also underlined in handwriting (or italicized in type).

When you write the title of a book, there are **two rules** you need to remember:

1. The first, the last, and all important words of a title are capitalized. Small words like *at, of, and, in, to, or,* and *the* are not capitalized.
2. The entire title is underlined.

Example: <u>Little House on the Prairie</u>

Since *on* and *the* are not the first words in the title and they are not important words, they are not capitalized.

Example: <u>The Secret Garden</u>

Since the word *the* is the first word in the title, it is capitalized.

PRACTICE EXERCISE 18.1

Directions: If the title is capitalized correctly, write *yes* on the line. If it is not capitalized correctly, write *no* on the line.

Example: How to Eat Fried Worms yes

1. Charlotte's web _____

2. Diary Of A Wimpy Kid _____

3. The Velveteen Rabbit _____

4. the Fellowship of the Ring _____

5. Pippi Longstocking _____

PRACTICE EXERCISE 18.2

Directions: Write each book title correctly on the line.

Example: the return of the Indian The Return of the Indian

1. tales of a fourth grade nothing _____

2. because of winn-dixie _____

3. frindle _____

4. freckle juice _____

5. little house in the big woods _____

6. the mouse and the motorcycle _____

7. the indian in the cupboard _____

8. i was a third grade spy _____

9. how to train your dragon _____

COMMAS IN A SERIES

Commas are used to separate things in a list.

A **series** is a list of three or more items in a sentence.

Example: Lisa served <u>cookies</u>, <u>cupcakes</u>, and <u>ice cream</u> at her party.

Add a comma after each item before the conjunction in a series. (Common conjunctions are *and, but,* and *or.*)

In the following sentences, the items in the series are italicized, and commas have been added after each item in the series before the conjunction.

Ella's four cats are named *Fluffy, Henry, Garfield,* and *Oliver*.

We bought *bananas, peanut butter, bread, milk,* and *orange juice* at the store.

After school, we went to the *park,* the *zoo,* and the *library*.

Kevin's hobbies include *sports, baking,* and *art*.

Some sentences can be combined by making lists.

Examples:

Ava has three favorite sports. She likes basketball. She likes baseball. She also likes golf.

Ava's favorite sports are basketball, baseball, and golf.

Edward baked some desserts. He baked cookies. He baked a cake. He baked brownies. He also baked pastries.

Edward baked cookies, a cake, brownies, and pastries.

Jared's jacket has blue stripes. It has orange stripes. It also has yellow stripes.

Jared's jacket has blue, orange, and yellow stripes.

PRACTICE EXERCISE 19.1

Directions: If commas are correctly used in the sentence, write *yes*. If not, write *no*.
Example: The cook can fry, broil, steam, and bake fish. <u>yes</u>

1. They served hamburgers hot dogs and, baked beans at the picnic. ___

2. You may have juice milk or water. _____

3. The decorations have red, yellow, and blue colors. _____

4. Please wash, dry, and put away the dishes. _____

5. We are having steak potatoes, and salad for dinner. _____

PRACTICE EXERCISE 19.2

Directions: Add commas where they belong in each sentence.
Example: Please buy milk, tomatoes, lettuce, and bread at the store.

1. We have vanilla cherry and strawberry yogurt.

2. What kinds of soups salads and sandwiches do you have?

3. Be sure to put forks spoons and knives on the table.

4. We looked at the apple lemon and pumpkin pies.

5. Is this pie filled with pudding apples or peaches?

6. I'd like toast eggs sausage and bacon for breakfast.

7. Jenny Lyle Olivia and Paulo are going to the concert.

8. They will hear country rock and classical music.

WRITING QUOTATIONS

Use **quotation marks** (" ") to show the exact words someone has spoken or written.

When you repeat the exact words that someone has spoken, you are quoting that person. The repeated words are called a **quotation**.

When you quote someone in writing, you should use quotation marks (" ").

There are two main ways to write a quotation.

At the beginning of a sentence:

"Thank you for walking with me," said Ben.

At the end of a sentence:

Ben said, "Thank you for walking with me."

Rules for writing quotations:

- Notice that the first word inside the quotation marks begins with a capital letter.
- A comma also separates the quotation from the rest of the sentence.
- The comma comes before the quotation marks.
- If the quotation is a question or an exclamation, a question mark or exclamation mark is used at the end of the quotation instead of a comma.

  - "What time does the movie start?" Ron asked.
  - Ron asked, "What time does the movie start?"
  - "I can't wait to see that movie!" Jessie exclaimed.
  - Jessie exclaimed, "I can't wait to see that movie!"

When you write quotations, try not to use the word *said* all the time. Use different words to make your writing more interesting. Try words like *whispered, muttered, replied, answered, remarked,* and *shouted.*

PRACTICE EXERCISE 20.1

Directions: Add quotation marks where they belong.
Example: "I can't find my baseball glove," said Barrett.

1. Will you let me use your markers? Tina asked.

2. Of course you can use them, Susan answered.

3. Matt's father shouted, Look at the shooting star!

4. I've never seen one before, Matt replied.

5. Angela asked, What time does the movie start?

PRACTICE EXERCISE 20.2

Directions: Add punctuation and quotation marks where they belong in each sentence.
Example: "Look at all the pretty flowers!" Jenna exclaimed.

1. Justice has a new puppy Grace said

2. When did he get it Emma asked

3. Grace replied He got it yesterday

4. She said It was a gift for his birthday

5. Was he excited Emma asked

6. Grace answered Yes, you should have seen the look on his face

7. Emma exclaimed Oh, look! Here he comes now with the new puppy

8. Grace asked Can we pet your puppy

SUBJECTS AND PREDICATES

Name _____ Date _____

Directions: It's time to **Roll and Mark** these complete predicates. First, roll one die. Find the number you rolled on the chart. Then complete that action for the first sentence. Repeat the process and work your way through the rest of the sentences. (You can write your new sentences on a separate sheet of paper.)

Number Rolled	Action	Number Rolled	Action
1	Draw a line between the complete subject and the complete predicate.	4	Underline the complete subject with a wavy line.
2	Use a highlighter to mark the complete subject.	5	Draw a box around the complete predicate.
3	Underline the complete predicate in red.	6	Choose any action from 1–5.

	Number Rolled	Sentences
1)		My grandparents bought a new washing machine.
2)		The canyon walls are extremely steep.
3)		The two brothers are washing dishes in the kitchen.
4)		Jeremy finished writing his report.
5)		An annoying fly buzzed around her head. .
6)		The weeds in the garden were difficult to pull.
7)		That cold lemonade tasted delicious!
8)		Treydon sanded and painted the chair.
9)		The basketball team won.
10)		The canoe tipped over in the lake.

PARTS OF SPEECH BINGO

Name _____ Date _____

Directions: Cut out the words at the top of the page. Turn them over and have someone randomly select one and read it out loud. Use a coin or crayon to mark a spot on the bingo board that matches the word being called. Once you have marked five spots in a row, you have a "bingo" and have won.

cupcake	school	sandwich	Mary	book	school
listen	talk	gallop	laugh	jump	write
dusty	pretty	slow	small	green	sweet
you	he	him	she	they	we
slowly	quietly	quickly	always	carefully	never
barn	speak	us	scary	softly	street

B	I	N	G	O
Noun	Verb	Adjective	Pronoun	Adverb
Verb	Adjective	Pronoun	Adverb	Noun
Pronoun	Adverb	FREE	Noun	Verb
Adverb	Noun	Verb	Adjective	Pronoun
Adjective	Pronoun	Adverb	Verb	Noun

PART 2

GRADE 4

COMPLETE SENTENCES

A **complete sentence** is a group of words that expresses a complete thought. It has a subject and a predicate.

Read each of the following groups of words. Think about which groups of words make sense by themselves. Those groups of words express complete thoughts and are sentences.

1. My parents bought a new couch.
2. A very hot day.
3. The two cousins.
4. They baked some delicious cookies.

Numbers 1 and 4 are complete sentences. Numbers 2 and 3 are not sentences. They do not express complete thoughts.

We can change numbers 2 and 3 to complete sentences by adding the missing subject or predicate:

1. *It is* a very hot day.
2. The two cousins *are washing the dishes*.

When you write a sentence, be sure it has both a subject and a predicate so that it is a complete sentence.

PRACTICE EXERCISE 1.1

Directions: Underline the group of words in each pair that is a sentence.

Example: <u>Jim has trained his dog to roll over.</u> Rolls over on the ground.

1. Difficult to find the plants. There are many weeds in the garden.

2. The canoe tipped over in the lake. Made a huge splash.

3. Laura and Rosie. The two friends made some lemonade.

4. The builders have been working hard. Building a new addition on the house.

5. My grandfather builds furniture. A talented carpenter.

PRACTICE EXERCISE 1.2

Directions: Write *sentence* or *not a sentence* for each group of words.

Example: In the days of dinosaurs. <u>not a sentence</u>

1. The canyon walls are very steep. _____

2. Hawaii has many beautiful beaches. _____

3. In the days of the pioneers. _____

4. Finished making the project. _____

5. My friend gave me a beautiful drawing. _____

6. Apple pie with vanilla ice cream. _____

7. Drinking the lemonade. _____

8. She remembered every detail of the story. _____

2

SENTENCE FRAGMENTS

A sentence is a group of words that expresses a complete thought. A **sentence fragment** is just a part of a sentence. It is missing a subject or a predicate and cannot stand by itself.

To change a sentence fragment to a complete sentence, you need to add either a subject or a predicate, depending on which is missing.

Here are some examples of sentence fragments. Following each sentence fragment is a correct complete sentence.

Sentence Fragment	Complete Sentence
Jumped for joy.	Sarah and Lisa jumped for joy.
Hit the baseball.	The batter hit the baseball.
My grandparents.	My grandparents went on vacation.
Fed the animals.	The zookeeper fed the animals.
The giraffes.	The giraffes ate the leaves.

2

PRACTICE EXERCISE 2.1

Directions: Note whether each group of words is a complete sentence or a sentence fragment.

Example: Went to the race. <u>sentence fragment</u>

1. The tired hikers rested at the edge of the lake. _____

2. My sister. _____

3. Solves crossword puzzles. _____

4. Elaine plays the saxophone and the trumpet. _____

5. Because she wanted to make a pie. _____

PRACTICE EXERCISE 2.2

Directions: Rewrite each sentence fragment so that it becomes a complete sentence.

Example: Ducks and geese. <u>Ducks and geese fly in flocks.</u>

1. The sky.

   _____

2. On the chairs by the pool.

   _____

3. Tied a ribbon on the package.

   _____

4. The cake in the oven.

   _____

RUN-ON SENTENCES

A **run-on sentence** is a group of words where two sentences are joined together without using correct punctuation. The multiple sentences in a run-on sentence run together without stopping or pausing where they should.

For example, this is a run-on sentence: John baked a pie Lily baked cupcakes.

You can correct a run-on sentence in different ways:

1. Separate the two sentences by adding a period and capitalizing the first word in the second sentence: John baked a pie. Lily baked cupcakes.
2. Add a comma and a conjunction (*and, but, or, so*) between the two sentences that run together: John baked a pie, and Lily baked cupcakes.

Here are some more examples of run-on sentences that have been corrected:

RUN-ON SENTENCE CORRECTIONS		
Run-On Sentence	**Corrected by Separation**	**Correction by Adding a Comma and Conjunction**
Many people went to the movie some people didn't like it.	Many people went to the movie. Some people didn't like it.	Many people went to the movie, but some people didn't like it.
The car stopped at the red light it started again when the light turned green.	The car stopped at the red light. It started again when the light turned green.	The car stopped at the red light, and it started again when the light turned green.

PRACTICE EXERCISE 3.1

Directions: Note whether each of the following sentences is a run-on sentence or a complete sentence.

Example: Maddy hit the baseball it went over the fence. run-on sentence

1. Football is a fun game it is exciting to play! _____

2. Today is a great day it is my birthday. _____

3. We went to the movie, and then we went home. _____

4. We laughed a lot it was a funny movie. _____

5. I wrote a poem, and it was beautiful. _____

PRACTICE EXERCISE 3.2

Directions: Fix each run-on sentence.

Example: The puppy followed me home it looked hungry.
The puppy followed me home. It looked hungry.

1. Mom called the car repair shop a nice lady answered.

   _____

2. The boy came to our house he thanked me for finding his dog.

   _____

3. The line was long we had to wait for 45 minutes.

   _____

4. Class ended early we got extra recess time.

   _____

SIMPLE SUBJECTS AND SIMPLE PREDICATES

The **simple subject** is the main word in the complete subject. The **simple predicate** is the main word or words in the complete predicate.

Remember that the **complete subject** is all the words in the subject part of the sentence. It tells who or what the sentence is about. The **complete predicate** is all the words in the predicate part of the sentence. It tells what the subject is or does.

Read the following five sentences. In each sentence, the complete subject is separated from the complete predicate with a | . The simple subject is underlined once, and the simple predicate is underlined twice.

1.   The basketball <u>team</u> | <u>has practiced</u> the new play for an hour.
2.   <u>Ms. Mahon</u> | <u>has</u> a new pair of glasses.
3.   The fifth-grade <u>class</u> | <u>ate</u> cupcakes at the party.
4.   A pesky <u>mosquito</u> | <u>buzzed</u> in my ear.
5.   <u>Leonard</u> | <u>has thrown</u> nine pitches so far.

Look at the sentences again. Most of the time the simple subject is just one word. Sometimes it is more than one word. In sentence 2, it is two words because it is a person's name.

Most of the time the simple predicate is also just one word. In sentences 1 and 5, it is two words because there is a helping verb with the main verb.

PRACTICE EXERCISE 4.1

Directions: The complete subject and complete predicate are separated by a | . Underline the simple subject once and the simple predicate twice.
Example: Our <u>team</u> | <u>has made</u> another touchdown.

1. His sprained wrist | began to swell.

2. A cactus | survives with very little water.

3. A warm jacket | feels nice on a cool day.

4. The state of California | is quite large.

5. The large deer | disappeared into the woods.

PRACTICE EXERCISE 4.2

Directions: Separate the complete subject and the complete predicate with a | . Underline the simple subject once and the simple predicate twice.
Example: The road <u>construction</u> | <u>slowed</u> traffic for hours.

1. The team captain encouraged his teammates to do better.

2. My sister always sings in the car.

3. The antelope ran across the open field.

4. Ben has entered the poetry contest.

5. The teacher prepared her lessons for the week.

6. The excited child screamed with delight on the ride.

7. The entire class went to the water park at the end of the school year.

COMPOUND SUBJECTS AND COMPOUND PREDICATES

A **compound subject** is two or more subjects that share a predicate. A **compound predicate** is two or more predicates that share a subject. Sometimes a sentence can have both a compound subject and a compound predicate.

Examples:

Justice and Noah | watched the show. (compound subject)

Grace | danced and sang in the talent show. (compound predicate)

My mom and dad | ran and swam in the race yesterday. (compound subject and compound predicate)

Notice in the preceding sentences that the words in a compound subject or predicate are often separated by the words *and* and *or*.

PRACTICE EXERCISE 5.1

Directions: Underline the compound subject.
Example: <u>Seagulls and pelicans</u> flew overhead.

1. <u>Children and adults</u> waited in line at the amusement park.

2. <u>Caramel apples and popcorn</u> were their favorite treats.

3. <u>Goats, deer, and rabbits</u> are my favorite animals at the petting zoo.

4. <u>Runners and bikers</u> competed in the race on Saturday.

5. <u>Kelly and Eric</u> wished they could go to the movie, too.

PRACTICE EXERCISE 5.2

Directions: Underline the compound predicate.
Example: The children <u>laughed and played</u> on the playground.

1. I <u>collect and sell</u> old postage stamps.

2. Jenny and Tralisa <u>painted and drew</u> all afternoon.

3. Rashanna <u>collects, paints, and decorates</u> rocks.

4. The fish in the river <u>swam and jumped</u>.

5. The musicians <u>sang and played</u> instruments during the concert.

COMPOUND SENTENCES

A **compound sentence** joins two or more simple sentences or **independent clauses** together with a coordinating conjunction. An **independent clause** is a phrase that can stand on its own as a complete thought.

An independent clause contains three things:

1. A subject (who or what the sentence is about)
2. A predicate (an action that the subject is doing)
3. A complete thought

You can join two independent clauses together to make a compound sentence. One way to do this is to connect the two sentences with a comma and a coordinating conjunction.

Example:

Keisha is going to the mall. She is going to the movies.

Keisha is going to the mall, *and* she is going to the movies.

There are seven coordinating conjunctions. You can remember them with the acronym **FANBOYS**:

For
And
Nor
But
Or
Yet
So

Here are some examples of compound sentences combined with coordinating conjunctions:

Troy likes to play basketball, *and* he has a game on Tuesday.

I can bake cookies, *but* I don't feel like baking today.

PRACTICE EXERCISE 6.1

Directions: Write *compound sentence* next to the sentences that are compound and *not a compound sentence* next to the sentences that are not compound.

Example: Dale felt nervous, but he kept moving toward the zip line. compound sentence

1. Henry had never been roller skating before. _____

2. Mom and Dad showed us some old photos. _____

3. Eva brought binoculars, and Sue used them to look for deer.

    _____

4. We looked out the window, but we couldn't see the amusement park yet. _____

5. It is a lot of fun to make apple pies and blueberry pies. _____

PRACTICE EXERCISE 6.2

Directions: Circle the coordinating conjunction and underline the independent clauses in each compound sentence.

Example: Matt had seen many animals in his life, but he had never seen a whale.

1. It was an exciting moment in the game, but it didn't last for long.

2. We hadn't found the roller coaster, but we kept looking.

3. It was hot outside, so she planned on going to the pool with her friends.

4. I can't wait to go to the zoo, and I plan on seeing the monkeys first.

5. The aquarium holds many different kinds of fish, and there are also many varieties of saltwater plants.

SIMPLE SUBJECTS

Name _____ Date _____

Directions: If the simple subject is correctly underlined, color the crayon green.
If the simple subject is incorrectly underlined, color the crayon orange.

Two <u>friends</u> watched the football game together.

Our math teacher <u>showed</u> us how to solve the problem.

<u>His</u> hobby is making model airplanes.

The <u>giraffe</u> ate leaves from the tree.

Mr. Severe has a new <u>pair</u> of glasses.

A <u>chameleon</u> blends in with its surrounding colors.

The basketball <u>team</u> practiced the new play.

<u>My</u> mother wrote the note on a sheet of yellow paper.

The <u>glass</u> vase shattered as it fell to the floor.

Eric <u>ate</u> a brownie sundae for dessert.

The rugged <u>football</u> player made the tackle.

<u>Michael</u> is always helpful and cheerful.

The <u>deer</u> jumped over the fence.

That orange <u>racecar</u> will probably win the race.

His <u>mountain</u> bike has a flat tire.

Thirty colorful <u>balloons</u> drifted up into the sky.

SIMPLE PREDICATES

Name _____ Date _____

WINTER | SPORTS | CAMPING | COOKIES | OCEANS

Directions: It's time to **Spin and Write!** Hold a pencil at the center of the spinner and thread a paper clip onto it. Spin the paper clip around the pencil to select a topic. Write a complete sentence about that topic on line 1. Then spin again and write a sentence on that topic on line 2. Repeat until you have written 10 sentences. Finally, highlight the simple predicate in each sentence.

	Topic	My Sentence
1)		
2)		
3)		
4)		
5)		
6)		
7)		
8)		
9)		
10)		

RELATIVE PRONOUNS

A **relative pronoun** is used to introduce a **relative clause**, which describes a noun.

For example:

This is the man *who* raked our leaves.

The word *who* is the relative pronoun. It introduces the relative clause *raked our leaves,* which gives more information about the man.

There are five main relative pronouns:

who   whom   whose   which   that

Relative Pronoun	Purpose	Example
who	gives information about people	Joe is the person who rescues animals.
whom	gives information about people	She is the person whom we need to thank.
whose	shows ownership	Ava is the girl whose costume won an award.
which	adds extra information about an object	The car, which has no windows, cannot be driven.
that	gives information about an object	We carved a pumpkin that was very large.

We use relative pronouns to relate descriptions to a noun in the sentence.

PRACTICE EXERCISE 7.1

Directions: Write a relative pronoun on the line to complete each sentence.

Example: The movie <u>that</u> I rented is about a sled dog.

1.   We saw the neighbor to _____ we had spoken earlier.

2.   We are going to the park _____ we visited last month.

3.   The cupcakes, _____ have no frosting, need to be decorated.

4.   The teacher, _____ students were in music class, worked on her lesson plans.

5.   Isn't Sadie the person _____ won the award?

PRACTICE EXERCISE 7.2

Directions: Circle the relative pronoun in each sentence.

Example: Our favorite restaurant, which serves pizza, is open until 9:00 in the evening.

1.   You are welcome to borrow the book that I read.

2.   My teacher, whom I admire, works hard every day.

3.   People who talk during the movies can be annoying.

4.   Lunar eclipses, which happen rarely, are amazing to see.

5.   My friend who lives next door is an incredible artist.

6.   The movie, which we watched yesterday, was quite scary.

7.   Mr. Hanson, whose son is a baseball player, was at the game.

8.   That woman who is wearing the green hat is my grandmother.

RELATIVE ADVERBS

A **relative adverb** introduces a group of words called a relative clause, which gives more information about a noun.

Example: Do you know of a park *where* we can walk our dog?

In the preceding example, the word *where* is the relative adverb. It introduces the relative clause *we can walk our dog,* which gives more information about the park.

There are three main relative adverbs:

where   when   why

Relative Adverb	Purpose	Example
where	gives information about a place	I wonder where they put the pumpkins.
when	gives information about a time	She was excited when it was time for the birthday party.
why	gives a reason	Leah wasn't sure why the plants had died.

We use relative adverbs to relate more information about a noun in a sentence.

Other relative adverbs include *how, whatever, whenever,* and *wherever.*

PRACTICE EXERCISE 8.1

Directions: Write a relative adverb on the line to complete each sentence.

Example: I love the time of year <u>when</u> my family gets together.

1. I wonder _____ the lights are on in the abandoned house.

2. That is the school _____ I learned to write poetry.

3. Friday is the day _____ we get extra recess time.

4. The house _____ my friend lives is not too far away.

5. Do you know _____ the restaurant closed?

PRACTICE EXERCISE 8.2

Directions: Circle the relative adverb in each sentence.

Example: What is the reason (why) the school dismissed students early?

1. That is why I go to the library so often.

2. She was looking forward to when the party would begin.

3. The place where the dinosaur bones were found is just a mile away.

4. This is the place where we will plant the garden.

5. Do you ever wonder why camels have humps on their backs?

6. It's almost time when we will have a snack.

7. That college is where she earned her teaching degree.

8. Do you know when the movie will begin?

LINKING VERBS

A **linking verb** shows being. It links the subject with a word or words in the predicate. A linking verb does not show action. It tells what the subject is, was, or will be.

You already know that an action verb shows action. It can tell what the subject does. Examples of action verbs include *run, hide, discuss, learn, eat, laugh,* and *howl.*

A verb can also show being.

Example: Her name *is* Macey O'Leary.

In the preceding sentence, the linking verb *is* links *Macey O'Leary* with the word *name.*

Use this chart to find and use common linking verbs.

LINKING VERBS			
am	is	are	was
were	be	been	has been
have been	become	might have been	might be
being	will be	appear	sound
look	grow	feel	get
remain	smell	stay	prove
seem	taste	turn	sit

PRACTICE EXERCISE 9.1

Directions: Circle the linking verb in each sentence.
Example: The light bulb (was) an important invention.

1. This package is a gift for you.

2. The runners were exhausted after the race.

3. The beach looks very crowded.

4. My friend seems quiet today.

5. This spaghetti is quite spicy.

PRACTICE EXERCISE 9.2

Directions: Circle the linking verb and underline the two words that the verb links.
Example: January (was) the coldest month of the year.

1. My aunt is a piano teacher.

2. The sky looks beautiful today.

3. Chocolate chip cookies taste wonderful.

4. The winter seems very long this year.

5. The sun feels warm on our faces.

6. Albany is the capital of New York.

7. We were excited to go canoeing.

8. Main Street is very busy.

MAIN VERBS AND HELPING VERBS

Main verbs show the main action in a sentence. **Helping verbs** help the main verb show its tense. They work with the main verbs to tell when an action happens.

Common helping verbs include *am, is, are, was, were, has, have, had,* and *will.*

In the following sentences, the main verb is underlined once, and the helping verb is underlined twice:

Sarah <u>will</u> <u>watch</u> the movie tonight.

Our friends <u>have</u> <u>arrived</u> for dinner.

My mother <u>has</u> <u>added</u> some spices to the sauce.

USING HELPING VERBS	
Rule	**Examples**
When the helping verb is *am, is, are, was,* or *were,* the main verb often ends with *-ing.*	I *am* listening. You *are* listening. They *were* listening.
When the helping verb is *has, have,* or *had,* the main verb often ends with *-ed.*	He *has* practiced. We *have* practiced. They *had* practiced.
When the helping verb is *will,* the main verb does not change.	She *will* watch the play. They *will* watch the play.

The helping verb is often found immediately before the main verb.

PRACTICE EXERCISE 10.1

Directions: Underline each main verb once. Underline each helping verb twice.

Example: The teacher <u>had</u> <u>helped</u> the student.

1. My father is painting the living room.

2. I am helping at the yard sale.

3. Alison is cooking spaghetti for dinner.

4. The group of friends had picked some cucumbers in the garden.

5. They will eat them in a salad at dinner.

PRACTICE EXERCISE 10.2

Directions: Complete each sentence by writing a helping verb on the line. Circle the main verb in each sentence.

Example: She will (need) some cinnamon in order to make the pie.

1. The family _____ invited twelve people to the party.

2. The book club _____ meet at the library tonight.

3. The sun _____ set in one hour.

4. Astronomers _____ discovered many new stars.

5. Brian _____ helping with the talent show.

6. We _____ earned enough money to buy a ticket to the zoo.

7. The class _____ chosen to have extra recess time as a reward.

8. Shelby _____ writing her biography.

11

PROGRESSIVE VERB TENSE

The **progressive verb tense** shows an ongoing or continuing action in progress.

There are three types of progressive verb tenses:

The **past progressive tense** shows events that lasted for a period of time in the past.

Example: I *was reading* my book for several hours.

The **present progressive tense** shows actions that are happening right now.

Example: Maria *is watching* a show.

The **future progressive tense** shows actions that will be happening in the future.

Example: They *will be running* in the race soon.

To correctly use the progressive verb tense, follow a "to be" verb with a verb ending with *-ing*.

USING PROGRESSIVE VERB TENSE			
	Past Progressive	**Present Progressive**	**Future Progressive**
How to Form This Tense	subject + *was/ were* + *-ing* verb	subject + *am/is/ are* + *-ing* verb	subject + *will be* + *-ing* verb
Examples	was talking	am talking	will be talking
	were eating	are eating	will be eating
	was playing	is playing	will be playing
	were going	are going	will be going
	was listening	am listening	will be listening

Sometimes a word can separate the "to be" verb from the -*ing* verb.

Example: Marley <u>is</u> *never* <u>watching</u> that movie again.

In the previous sentence, the word *never* separates *is* from *watching*.

PRACTICE EXERCISE 11.1

Directions: Write the progressive verb tense used in each sentence.
Example: Mr. Jones <u>is taking</u> his daily walk. <u>present progressive</u>

1. Janice <u>was listening</u> to her teacher. _____

2. We <u>will be eating</u> cake later tonight. _____.

3. The students <u>are working</u> on their projects. _____

4. All of the players <u>were practicing</u> on the field. _____

5. They <u>will be playing</u> in a game tonight. _____

PRACTICE EXERCISE 11.2

Directions: Complete the table by writing the progressive tenses for each verb. The first row is filled in as an example.

PROGRESSIVE VERB TENSE		
Past Progressive	**Present Progressive**	**Future Progressive**
subject + *was/were* + *-ing* verb	subject + *am/is/are* + *-ing* verb	subject + *will be* + *-ing* verb
was thinking	am thinking	will be thinking
were washing		
		will be enjoying
	are spending	
was looking		
	is wishing	
		will be painting

RUN-ON SENTENCES

Name _____ Date _____

Directions: It's time to **Roll and Repair** these run-on sentences. First, roll one die. Find the number you rolled on the chart. Then complete that action for the first sentence. Repeat the process and work your way through the rest of the sentences. (You can write your new sentences on a separate sheet of paper.)

Number Rolled	Action	Number Rolled	Action
1	Make two complete sentences by separating the run-on.	4	Color the sentence's box red.
2	Underline a part of the run-on that could be a complete sentence by itself.	5	Draw a green line to separate the two smaller sentences.
3	Make a complete sentence by adding a word or words.	6	Choose any action from 1–5.

	Number Rolled	Run-On Sentence
1)		The dog was running in circles it made us laugh.
2)		My friends paddled the canoe it tipped over.
3)		Jenny loves funny movies she is going to see one tonight.
4)		Our aunt is going on a trip she is going to Alaska.
5)		Ava is making the sugar cookies Lisa is frosting them.
6)		They started the campfire they set up their tent.
7)		We are making candy later it will be delicious.
8)		My sister is graduating from school she is going to college.
9)		Tristan studied for the test he didn't miss one problem.
10)		They were late for dinner the food was cold.

ADJECTIVE CATEGORIES

An **adjective** is a word that describes a noun. There are many types of adjectives, and each adjective belongs to a **category**.

There are many categories of adjectives, as shown in the following chart.

ADJECTIVE CATEGORIES			
Number/ Quantity	**Opinion**	**Size**	**Shape**
five	beautiful	gigantic	round
two	horrible	wide	crooked
three hundred	lovely	skinny	flat
first	adorable	enormous	circular
third	magnificent	heavy	square
Condition	**Age**	**Color**	**Pattern**
broken	young	pastel	striped
guilty	old	silver	plaid
rich	elderly	turquoise	spotted
famous	teenage	transparent	checkered
sleepy	antique	blue	flowered

ADJECTIVE CATEGORIES			
Origin	**Material**	**Type**	**Purpose**
American	cloth	all-purpose	swimming (pool)
Japanese	plastic	part-time	sports (car)
southern	cotton	time-saving	dining (table)
western	silk	heavy-duty	running (shoes)
British	leather	last-minute	sewing (machine)

By using a variety of adjectives from different categories, you can create a specific image for your reader.

Examples:

The puppies ran down the road.

Three adorable, tired brown puppies ran down the spooky, wide road.

Try using more adjectives from different categories to improve your own writing.

12

PRACTICE EXERCISE 12.1

Directions: Note which category each adjective belongs to.
Example: exhausted <u>condition</u>

1. flaky _____

2. curved _____

3. young _____

4. miniature _____

5. many _____

PRACTICE EXERCISE 12.2

Directions: Underline the adjective(s) in each sentence and tell
which category it belongs to.
Example: Dr. White won an award for her <u>amazing</u> scientific
research. <u>opinion</u>

1. The tired skater drank some hot chocolate. _____

2. She threw the ball to the excited puppy. _____

3. We went to a Mexican restaurant for dinner. _____

4. The deer ran across the wide meadow. _____

5. Charity picked twelve roses. _____

6. Wild geese flew over the lake. _____

7. She ate the delicious cookies. _____

8. I ate a sour pickle. _____

WHAT IS AN ADJECTIVE?

Name _____ Date _____

Directions: It's time to **Spin and Write!** Hold a pencil at the center of the spinner and thread a paper clip onto it. Spin the paper clip around the pencil to select an adjective category. Write that category and an adjective for that category on the first line. Then spin again and write an adjective for that category on line 2. Repeat until you have written 19 adjectives. An example is provided for you.

COLOR

SHAPE ● SIZE

OPINION

Category	Adjective
opinion	gorgeous

Category	Adjective

81

ADJECTIVE ORDER

When more than one adjective is used to describe a noun, all the adjectives need to be listed in the correct order.

The following table shows the correct order of adjective categories.

ORDER OF ADJECTIVES		
Order	**Category**	**Examples**
1	number	four, three hundred, third, first, last
2	opinion	pretty, expensive, gorgeous, difficult, easy
3	size	big, little, small, tiny, large, enormous
4	shape	round, square, flat, wide, narrow
5	condition	cold, empty, hungry, rich, messy
6	age	new, young, modern, old, antique
7	color	yellow, gold, silver, pink, transparent
8	origin	French, American, Italian, Mexican, British
9	materials	gold, silver, leather, cotton, paper
10	purpose	sleeping (bag), hunting (dog), frying (pan)

Placing adjectives in the correct order helps the sentence to make sense. Use the correct order when there is more than one adjective used to describe a noun.

For example, this sentence does not sound right because the adjectives are in the wrong order:

The hot, sweet, three chocolate chip cookies tasted delicious.

The adjective *three* should come before the other adjectives:

The three hot, sweet chocolate chip cookies tasted delicious.

PRACTICE EXERCISE 13.1

Directions: If the adjectives are in the correct order, write *yes*. If not, write *no*.
Example: green, tall plant <u>no</u>

1. new, many cars _____

2. orange, round pumpkins _____

3. new, yellow house _____

4. salty, round crackers _____

PRACTICE EXERCISE 13.2

Directions: Write three adjectives to describe each noun. Be sure to write them in the correct order.
Example: <u>four</u>, <u>delicious</u>, <u>round</u> rolls

1. _____, _____, _____ flowers

2. _____, _____, _____ car

3. _____, _____, _____ house

PREPOSITIONS

A **preposition** is a word that relates a noun or pronoun to another word in the sentence.

In the following sentences, the italicized words are prepositions:

The students cut out pictures *of* animals.

The caterpillar was *on* the branch.

The skier drank some hot cocoa *from* a mug.

She put the candy *in* a bag.

Each preposition gives additional information about the noun it follows.

There are many different prepositions.

THIRTY COMMON PREPOSITIONS				
about	above	across	after	around
at	before	behind	below	beside
by	down	during	for	from
in	inside	near	of	off
on	out	outside	over	through
to	under	up	with	without

A preposition often tells where something is located in relation to another object.

Example: The family slept in a tent.

In the previous sentence, the word *in* connects the noun *family* with the noun *tent*. It tells **where** the family slept.

PRACTICE EXERCISE 14.1

Directions: Circle the preposition in each sentence.
Example: The sun always sets (in) the west.

1. We waited a long time at the office.

2. I found my book under the couch.

3. A breeze blew the papers off the desk.

4. She rode her bike down the path.

5. Kelly took pictures with her new camera.

PRACTICE EXERCISE 14.2

Directions: Write a preposition on the line to complete each sentence.
Example: The bowl fell off the counter.

1. Karen takes karate lessons _____ school.

2. I was happy _____ my grades.

3. We read a story _____ a lonely dog.

4. We bought a present _____ my sister.

5. Boil the spaghetti _____ ten minutes.

6. The plane soared _____ the clouds.

7. The batter hit the baseball _____ the fence.

8. We walked _____ the pond.

PREPOSITIONAL PHRASES

A **prepositional phrase** includes the preposition, the object, and all the words between them.

Remember that a preposition shows the relationship between a noun or pronoun and another word in a sentence. A prepositional phrase begins with the preposition.

Read the following sentences. The prepositional phrase is highlighted. The preposition is underlined once, and the object of the preposition is underlined twice.

Mindy sat on the blue couch.

We ate a picnic lunch at the neighborhood park.

Place the dirty dishes in the sink.

The kitten ran out the front door.

A jet could be seen above the clouds.

Notice that each prepositional phrase begins with a preposition, ends with an object, and includes all words in between.

Here are some examples of prepositional phrases:

behind the box	over the desk
into the woods	on the mountainside
in the car	from his friend

Use prepositional phrases to add more detail to your sentences when writing.

PRACTICE EXERCISE 15.1

Directions: Underline the prepositional phrase in each sentence.
Example: Please bring me some cookies <u>without any frosting</u>.

1. I climbed carefully up the ladder.

2. The reporter wrote a story about the event.

3. We waited a long time at the gate.

4. Jessica found her glasses under the couch.

5. The cousins will visit during summer vacation.

PRACTICE EXERCISE 15.2

Directions: Underline each prepositional phrase. Circle the preposition and draw an arrow to the object.
Example: Lyle left his tennis racket (at) <u>the park</u>.

1. Charles goes camping in the forest.

2. They ate their dinner before the game.

3. I studied hard at school.

4. The bride walked down the aisle.

5. Did you know they are building a museum across the street?

6. There was a tiny kitten sitting between the two girls.

7. We walked around the river bend.

8. The log flume ride took us through a dark tunnel.

COMMONLY CONFUSED WORDS

Some words, such as *to*, *two*, and *too*, can be confusing. It is important to know the difference so that you can use them correctly.

Use the following chart to learn the differences between words that are commonly confused.

COMMONLY CONFUSED WORDS		
Word	**Meaning**	**Example**
two	a number	We need **two** eggs for the cookies.
to	toward	Are you going **to** the concert?
too	also or much	Can we go, **too**?
there	a place	Put the book over **there**.
their	owned by them	Listen to **their** story.
they're	they are	**They're** watching the movie.
its	owned by it	The cat chased **its** tail.
it's	it is	**It's** a beautiful day outside.
can	shows ability, able to	Lily **can** draw beautifully.
may	shows permission	You **may** draw a picture.
your	owned by you	Try to finish **your** homework early.
you're	you are	Let me know when **you're** finished.
by	near or beside	Please place the pie **by** the ice cream.
bye	goodbye	"**Bye**," she said as she left the room.
buy	to purchase	I need to **buy** some new shoes.

PRACTICE EXERCISE 16.1

Directions: If the underlined word is used correctly, write *yes*.
If not, write *no*.
Example: <u>It's</u> almost time for the movie to start. <u>yes</u>

1. I need to <u>bye</u> some groceries today. _____

2. Do you see the deer in the field over <u>their</u>? _____

3. <u>It's</u> a rainy day today. _____

4. <u>You're</u> the best! _____

5. Please give the gift <u>to</u> your teacher. _____

PRACTICE EXERCISE 16.2

Directions: Underline the word that best completes each sentence.
Example: I am going (two, <u>to</u>, too) the fair.

1. (Their, They're, There) asking for donations for the animal shelter.

2. The dog hurt (its, it's) paw.

3. Are you going to get (you're, your) hair cut this afternoon?

4. Please put the forks (by, buy, bye) the napkins.

5. (It's, Its) time for the play to begin.

6. Make sure you give the book back (two, too, to) the library.

7. Put the games on the shelf over (their, they're, there).

8. (Your, You're) a great reader!

TITLES OF WORKS

A **title** is the specific name of a book, article, poem, show, song, or other work.

Titles can be capitalized, appear in quotation marks, or be italicized (or underlined, if handwritten), depending on the type of title.

Follow these rules for correctly writing titles.

WRITING TITLES		
Medium	**Format**	**Example**
Book	Italicize or Underline	J. K. Rowling wrote <u>Harry Potter and the Sorcerer's Stone</u>.
Poem or Short Story	Quotation Marks	We read the poem "The Road Not Taken" by Robert Frost.
Television Show	Italicize or Underline	*Arthur* is my favorite show. <u>Arthur</u> is my favorite show.
Article	Quotation Marks	The article "Nationals Win the World Series" was published in the sports magazine.
Play	Italicize	Our fourth-grade class is putting on the play *Charlotte's Web*.
Song	Quotation Marks	"Old McDonald Had a Farm" is my favorite song.
Magazine	Italicize	Do you ever read the magazine *Sports Illustrated for Kids*?

Note that you should capitalize the first letter of the first word, the last word, and all other important words in titles.

PRACTICE EXERCISE 17.1

Directions: Note whether each title is correctly written by writing *yes* or *no* on the line.
Example: Book: <u>Where the Red Fern Grows</u> <u>yes</u>

1. Poem: Still I Rise _____

2. Short Story: "The Tell-Tale Heart" _____

3. Magazine: *National Geographic* _____

4. Song: A Mother's Lullaby _____

5. Book: "Black Beauty" _____

PRACTICE EXERCISE 17.2

Directions: Correctly write each title.
Example: Song: "The Wagon Train"

1. Book: Bridge to Terabithia _____

2. Article: How to Bake Cookies _____

3. Song: Three Blind Mice _____

4. Book: Because of Winn-Dixie _____

5. Poem: Mother to Son _____

6. Magazine: The Farmer's Almanac _____

COMMAS IN QUOTATIONS

Remember that you should use **quotation marks** (" ") to show the exact words someone has said.

When you repeat the exact words that someone has spoken or written, you are quoting that person. The repeated words are called a **quotation**.

When you quote someone in writing, you should use quotation marks (" "). Often, there is a comma in or near the quotation marks.

Remember that there are two main ways to write a quotation.

At the beginning of a sentence:

Example: "Let's go to the swimming pool," said Horatio.

At the end of a sentence:

Example: Horatio said, "Let's go to the swimming pool."

Rules for writing quotations:

- The first word inside the quotation marks begins with a capital letter.
- A **comma separates** the quotation from the rest of the sentence.
- The **comma** comes **before** the quotation marks.
- If the quotation is a question or an exclamation, a question mark or exclamation mark is used at the end of the quotation instead of a comma.

Examples:

"When are we making the cookies?" Ari asked.

Ari asked, "When are we making the cookies?"

"Look at that huge wave!" Nicole exclaimed.

Nicole exclaimed, "Look at that huge wave!"

PRACTICE EXERCISE 18.1

Directions: Add quotation marks where they belong in each sentence.
Example: Bailey said, "You'll never guess what I made."

1.   Julie replied, No, that isn't my scarf.

2.   Duane said, I was never more surprised in my life.

3.   Will you please answer the phone? asked James.

4.   Thank you so much, said Stephanie.

5.   Keisha said, Let's go to the park today.

PRACTICE EXERCISE 18.2

Directions: Add punctuation and quotation marks where they belong in each sentence.
Example: "Your posters for the concert are beautiful!" Lila exclaimed.

1.   Our teacher said Take out your notebooks before class

2.   My mom stated We are having pizza for dinner

3.   Which circus act did you like best asked Gabe

4.   How did you train your dog to speak asked Kelsey

5.   She replied I used a lot of treats.

6.   Ava exclaimed I really love ice cream

7.   Joshua said Let's get ready to go to the movie

8.   Olivia shouted Watch out for the waves

COMMAS AND COORDINATING CONJUNCTIONS

Remember that a **conjunction** is a word that joins together other words, phrases, or parts of sentences.

The three most-used conjunctions are *and, or,* and *but.*

You can use coordinating conjunctions to join two simple sentences to create a compound sentence.

Example: Do you want vanilla ice cream, *or* would you prefer chocolate ice cream?

Notice that the comma comes directly **before** the conjunction used to join together the two sentences.

Look at the following compound sentences. Notice where the comma and the coordinating conjunction are in each sentence:

Jenny ate cookies, *and* I ate cupcakes.

There are many students in the school, *but* there is only one principal.

We brought bait with us, *and* we went fishing.

They can travel to the city by train, *or* they can take the bus.

I wanted to play checkers, *but* my brother wanted to play chess.

PRACTICE EXERCISE 19.1

Directions: Underline the coordinating conjunction in each compound sentence. Place a comma in front of each conjunction.
Example: Alex loves painting, <u>but</u> he doesn't like drawing.

1. Would you like apples or do you prefer pears?

2. I didn't feel well but I still went to work.

3. I had to clean my bedroom so I ran out of time to do my homework.

4. Earth has one moon but Mars has two moons.

5. I went to the park and I played on the swings.

PRACTICE EXERCISE 19.2

Directions: Write a coordinating conjunction to complete each sentence. Place a comma where it belongs in each sentence.
Example: Will you go to the movie, <u>or</u> will you go skating?

1. It is raining _____ we will stay inside for recess.

2. I'm going to paint my room tonight _____ I might not have time to finish it.

3. Anne doesn't enjoy playing the piano _____ she is very good at it.

4. Manuel went to school _____ he took the test.

5. Liam wanted to go to an Italian restaurant _____ he wanted to eat at home.

6. Jerry's birthday is in May _____ mine is in October.

7. My mom needed some sugar _____ she added it to the shopping list.

PROOFREADING

Proofreading is when you read a passage and find and mark mistakes that have been made. It is an important step to improving your writing.

Use proofreading marks and symbols to make the job easier.

¶ Indent for new paragraph	≡ Capitalize
∧ Insert a word	/ Use lowercase
⊙ Insert a period	◯ Check spelling

The following sentences have several mistakes. Notice how the mistakes have been marked with proofreading marks.

she rewards her dog for following her commands

Corrected sentence:

She rewards her dog for following her commands.

On tuesday, our class is going to the philadelphia zoo.

Corrected sentence:

On Tuesday, our class is going to the Philadelphia Zoo.

Mr. jones is planning to bring an umbrella and a sell phone

Corrected sentence:

Mr. Jones is planning to bring an umbrella and a cell phone.

The next time you write a paragraph or an essay, try looking for mistakes and using proofreading marks to improve your final copy.

PRACTICE EXERCISE 20.1

Directions: Use proofreading marks to identify the mistakes in the sentence. Then write the sentence correctly on the line.

Your not going to be able to see the Show if you dont where you're glasses

_____

_____

PRACTICE EXERCISE 20.2

Directions: Use proofreading marks to mark all the mistakes in the paragraph. Then write the paragraph correctly on the lines.

many people like to have pets as they're companions. Having a pet, though, is not always easie. You have to tack good care of you're pet and make sure that it has plentie of food and watur you also have to take it outside for a walk everie day. Haveing a pet is a big responsibilitie

_____

_____

_____

_____

_____

_____

_____

_____

CONJUNCTIONS

Name _____ Date _____

Directions: If the word is a coordinating conjunction, color the apple green. If it is not a coordinating conjunction, color the apple red.

for	the	an	so
by	and	with	yet
yet	around	nor	near
speak	or	tree	but

PARTS OF SPEECH BINGO

Name _____ Date _____

Directions: Cut out the words at the top of the page. Turn them over and have someone randomly select one and read it out loud. Use coins or crayon to mark a spot on the bingo board that matches the word being called. Once you have marked five spots in a row, you have a "bingo" and have won.

who	whom	whose	which	that	am
is	are	was	were	be	been
has been	have been	become	being	will be	about
during	over	under	near	with	from
silly	sweet	kind	amazing	pretty	tall
house	girl	tree	desk	pretzel	pie

B	I	N	G	O
Noun	Linking Verb	Adjective	Relative Pronoun	Preposition
Linking Verb	Adjective	Relative Pronoun	Preposition	Noun
Relative Pronoun	Preposition	FREE	Noun	Linking Verb
Preposition	Noun	Linking Verb	Adjective	Relative Pronoun
Adjective	Relative Pronoun	Preposition	Linking Verb	Noun

PART 3

GRADE 5

POSSESSIVE NOUNS

A **possessive noun** shows ownership. It is a noun that owns or possesses another object.

Remember that a noun names a person, place, thing, or idea. In the following sentences, the italicized word is a possessive noun. It owns something.

1. *Jaylyn's* grandfather came to visit.
2. All the *carpenters'* hammers were busy pounding nails into the building.
3. The *children's* laughter echoed across the playground.

In sentence 1, the possessive noun is singular. The grandfather belongs to Jaylyn.

In sentence 2, the possessive noun is plural. The hammers belong to more than one carpenter.

In sentence 3, the possessive noun is plural. The laughter belongs to the children.

This chart explains how to form possessive nouns.

FORMING POSSESSIVE NOUNS		
To make the possessive of	**Add**	**Example**
a singular noun	's	lion's mane, tiger's tail
a plural noun ending in *s*	'	dogs' collars, flowers' petals
a plural noun not ending in *s*	's	men's jackets, geese's wings

PRACTICE EXERCISE 1.1

Directions: Underline the possessive noun in each sentence. Circle the object owned by the possessive noun.

Example: The horses' (hooves) sounded like thunder.

1. We went to the twins' birthday party. _____

2. These knives' blades need to be sharpened. _____

3. My dress's sleeve is torn. _____

4. The players' uniforms are blue and white. _____

5. John's bicycle has a flat tire. _____

PRACTICE EXERCISE 1.2

Directions: Write the possessive form of each noun.

Example: flower flower's

1. leader _____

2. coach _____

3. men _____

4. coaches _____

5. carpenters _____

6. balloon _____

7. faces _____

8. friend _____

USING IRREGULAR VERBS

Irregular verbs are verbs whose past tense you cannot form by adding *-ed*. Some irregular verbs follow a pattern in the way they are formed.

Some irregular verbs follow a pattern to make the past tense and the past participle. The following irregular verbs are grouped together by patterns to help you remember them.

Some verbs have the same past and past participle:

Present	Past	Past Participle
bring	brought	(has, have, had) brought
catch	caught	(has, have, had) caught
find	found	(has, have, had) found

Some verbs form the past participle by adding *-n* to the past tense:

Present	Past	Past Participle
break	broke	(has, have, had) broken
choose	chose	(has, have, had) chosen
freeze	froze	(has, have, had) frozen

Some verbs change one vowel in the past tense and past participle:

Present	Past	Past Participle
drink	drank	(has, have, had) drunk
ring	rang	(has, have, had) rung
sing	sang	(has, have, had) sung

PRACTICE EXERCISE 2.1

Directions: The present tense and past tense are given. Write the past participle of each verb.
Example: catch, caught, <u>(has, have, had) caught</u>

1. choose, chose, _____

2. find, found, _____

3. sing, sang, _____

4. break, broke, _____

5. think, thought, _____

PRACTICE EXERCISE 2.2

Directions: Write the past tense and past participle for each verb. The first row is filled in as an example.

Present	Past	Past Participle
bring	brought	(has, have, had) brought
break		
drink		
sing		
choose		
catch		
say		

VERBS WITH DIRECT OBJECTS

A **direct object** receives the action of the verb.

The direct object is a part of the complete predicate. It comes after an action verb and is usually a noun. The direct object answers the questions "whom?" or "what?"

In the following sentences, the italicized nouns are direct objects.

Our family eats *dinner* together.
(What does the family eat? Or, Our family eats what together?)

The lifeguard rescued the *swimmer*.
(Whom did the lifeguard rescue? Or, The lifeguard rescued whom?)

Carrie read a *book*.
(What did Carrie read? Or, Carrie read what?)

You can find the direct object in most sentences by asking yourself to what or to whom the action happens.

For example, in this sentence, the verb is *wrapped*: I *wrapped* the gift in green paper.

Ask yourself, "What did I wrap?" The answer is "I wrapped the gift." So *gift* is the direct object.

I wrapped the *gift* in green paper.

PRACTICE EXERCISE 3.1

Directions: The verb in each sentence is underlined. Draw an arrow from the verb to the direct object.

Example: The snow covered my window.

1. A thermometer <u>measures</u> the temperature.

2. The kitten <u>chased</u> its tail all morning.

3. Liselle <u>invited</u> the teacher to the meeting.

4. I <u>finished</u> my homework as quickly as possible.

5. Edward <u>changed</u> the tire on the truck.

PRACTICE EXERCISE 3.2

Directions: Underline the verb once. Underline the direct object twice.

Example: My mother <u>cooked</u> <u>dinner</u> for our entire family.

1. The weatherman predicted a large snowstorm.

2. The scientists studied the habits of wolves.

3. My sister brought eight pencils.

4. Ava chose a large balloon for her souvenir.

5. After the parade, Olivia drank some hot cocoa.

6. She broke the record at the race.

7. All the campers brought lunches for the hike.

8. They sang my favorite song last night!

USING THE PRESENT TENSE

A verb in the present tense must agree with the subject of a sentence.

Remember that linking verbs include the word *be* and other forms of *be*, such as *am, is, are, was,* and *were.* Different forms of *be* are used with different subjects.

You wouldn't say, "I *be* tired today." You would say, "I *am* tired today."
You wouldn't say, "Dogs *am* cute." You would say, "Dogs *are* cute."

When the correct verb form is used, we say that the subject and verb *agree.*

With a singular noun, use *-s* or *-es*:

A flash flood *occurs* in the desert.

Josh *catches* fish at the pond.

With a plural noun, do not use *-s* or *-es*:

Flash floods *occur* in the desert.

The boys *catch* fish at the pond.

With the singular pronouns *he, she,* or *it,* use *-s* or *-es*:

She *likes* to bake cakes.

He *mashes* the potatoes.

With *I, you, we,* or *they,* do not use *-s* or *-es*:

We *like* to bake cakes.

They *mash* the potatoes.

PRACTICE EXERCISE 4.1

Directions: Underline the word in parentheses that correctly completes each sentence.
Example: Pepper always (make, <u>makes</u>) me sneeze.

1. The chefs (use, uses) as little salt as possible.

2. The dancer (perform, performs) a beautiful ballet dance.

3. A cactus (need, needs) very little water to survive.

4. Our dogs (wake, wakes) us every morning.

5. She always (wear, wears) a life vest when she is in the boat.

PRACTICE EXERCISE 4.2

Directions: Write the correct present-tense form of the verb in parentheses.
Example: The boat <u>leaves</u> in one hour. (leave)

1. I _____ a flock of seagulls. (see)

2. Worms _____ a tasty meal for robins. (provide)

3. My coat _____ me warm all winter long. (keep)

4. They _____ their eyes during the scary parts of the movie. (cover)

5. Sea otters _____ a lot. (play)

6. He _____ the field to play baseball. (use)

7. The ducks' webbed feet _____ them to swim easily. (help)

8. That blue fish _____ to the ocean floor. (dive)

PERFECT VERB TENSE

The **perfect verb tense** is used to show a completed or perfected action. There are three perfect tenses: present perfect, past perfect, and future perfect.

Verbs in the perfect tense use a form of *have* or *had* followed by the past participle.

Past perfect: He *had finished* his homework an hour before the show.

Present perfect: He *has finished* his homework already.

Future perfect: He *will have finished* his homework by the time supper is ready.

You can decide which perfect verb tense to use by when the action occurred.

Past perfect: An action occurred before another event in the past.

Present perfect: An action occurred at an unspecified time in the past.

Future perfect: An action will occur before another event in the future.

PRACTICE EXERCISE 5.1

Directions: Underline the perfect tense verb in each sentence.
Example: She <u>had thought</u> about buying a basketball long before she ever bought one.

1.   He had been reading about how to build a campfire.

2.   By the end of the week, she will have watched two episodes of the show.

3.   She has been practicing her dance routine all week.

4.   By next year, they will have gone camping several times.

5.   Going on a cruise has been a goal of hers for a long time.

PRACTICE EXERCISE 5.2

Directions: Note whether the underlined verb is in the past perfect, the present perfect, or the future perfect tense.
Example: Joshua had tried a new dessert. <u>past perfect</u>

1.   By the end of the race, he <u>will have run</u> three miles. _____

2.   Lila <u>had looked</u> at the phone many times before she bought it. _____

3.   She <u>had worn</u> her shoes every day for a year before buying a new pair. _____

4.   By this time next year, they <u>will have read</u> many books. _____

5.   We <u>have been making</u> cookies with that recipe for years. _____

6.   She <u>has worn</u> that jacket for several months. _____

7.   Jake <u>had run</u> on the trails several times before. _____

TROUBLESOME VERB PAIRS

People often confuse and incorrectly use some verb pairs.

Can and *may* are often confused. *Sit* and *set* are also used incorrectly much of the time.

Use the verb *can* to mean "to be able to do something." Use the verb *may* when you ask or give permission.

Examples:

Can you reach that window? (Are you able to reach that window?)

May I show you how? (Do I have permission to show you how?)

Use the verb *sit* to mean "to rest." Use the verb *set* to mean "to put or place something."

Examples:

Please sit down and watch the show. (Please rest in a seat and watch the show.)

Where should I set the popcorn? (Where should I put the popcorn?)

PRACTICE EXERCISE 6.1

Directions: Underline the verb in parentheses that correctly completes each sentence.
Example: Did you (sit, set) your cake on the table? <u>set</u>

1. Is there anyone here who (can, may) blow up these balloons?

2. Where should everyone (sit, set) at the table?

3. (Can, May) I taste the cake now?

4. You (can, may) borrow the deck of cards.

5. Please (sit, set) the book on my desk.

PRACTICE EXERCISE 6.2

Directions: Use *can, may, sit,* or *set* to complete each sentence.
Example: The magician <u>can</u> fool the audience every time.

1. If you _____ here, you can see the show.

2. You _____ begin eating.

3. _____ I borrow your game tonight?

4. Where should we _____ for dinner?

5. You _____ leave the table when you are finished.

6. Michael, _____ you reach that dish in the cupboard?

7. If you _____ it on the edge of the counter, it will fall.

8. Please don't _____ a place for me at the table.

SPELLING VERBS CORRECTLY

The spelling of some verbs changes when you add -ed or -es.

Remember that the past tense of a verb is usually formed by adding -ed. The present tense is sometimes formed by adding -s or -es.

For example, to write a sentence using the present tense of the verb try, we could say, "She tries on her costume." To refer to the same event in the past tense, we would say, "She tried on her costume."

If the verb ends in a consonant and y, change the y to i before adding -es or -ed.

Examples:

apply, applies, applied

worry, worries, worried

If the verb has one syllable and ends in a vowel and a consonant, double the final consonant before adding -ed.

Examples:

hop, hops, hopped

plan, plans, planned

PRACTICE EXERCISE 7.1

Directions: Note whether each group of verbs is spelled correctly.
Example: worry, worrys, worryd <u>no</u>

1. study, studys, studyed _____

2. stub, stubs, stubbed _____

3. hurry, hurries, hurryed _____

4. plan, plans, planned _____

5. spy, spys, spied _____

PRACTICE EXERCISE 7.2

Directions: Write the correct past tense form of each verb.
Example: trip <u>tripped</u>

1. worry _____

2. carry _____

3. sip _____

4. supply _____

5. tan _____

6. tug _____

7. pry _____

8. slam _____

SUBJECT PRONOUNS

Some pronouns take the place of a noun as the subject of a sentence. These **subject pronouns** are *I, you, he, she, it, we,* and *they*.

In the first sentence of each of the following pairs, the subject is italicized. In the second sentence of each pair, the subjects has been replaced with a subject pronoun, also italicized.

Joe and Eric went to the amusement park.

They went to the amusement park.

Ms. Smith made a delicious apple pie.

She made a delicious apple pie.

The pronoun *I* is always capitalized. Use the following chart to identify the singular and plural subject pronouns.

SUBJECT PRONOUNS		
Singular	**Plural**	**Purpose**
I	we	talking about yourself
you	you	talking to someone else
he, she, it	they	talking about another person or thing or other people or things

PRACTICE EXERCISE 8.1

Directions: Underline the subject pronoun.
Example: <u>You</u> can go to the movies for half price on Tuesdays.

1. He forgot to buy snacks for the trip.

2. After dinner, we will visit a friend down the street.

3. It fell off the table and broke.

4. You need to see the photos from the trip to Africa.

5. I am so tired!

PRACTICE EXERCISE 8.2

Directions: Replace each underlined subject with a subject pronoun.
Example: <u>Joyce</u> found a book on the bench. <u>She</u>

1. <u>Max</u> drew a square on his paper. _____

2. <u>The boys</u> mowed three lawns this afternoon. _____

3. <u>Lisa</u> told a funny story. _____

4. <u>Our favorite show</u> is on tonight. _____

5. <u>The sleeping bag</u> is made for cold temperatures. _____

6. <u>Ms. Lee</u> asked the class a question. _____

7. <u>Gabriel</u> wasn't sure of the answer. _____

8. <u>Trey and I</u> had to hurry to catch the bus. _____

SUBJECT PRONOUNS

Name _____ Date _____

Spinner:
- I
- YOU
- HE OR SHE
- WE
- THEY

Directions: It's time to **Spin and Write!** Hold a pencil at the center of the spinner and thread a paper clip onto it. Spin the paper clip around the pencil to select a subject pronoun. Write a complete sentence using that pronoun on line 1. Then spin again and write a sentence using that pronoun on line 2. Repeat until you have written 10 sentences. Finally, highlight the subject pronoun in each sentence.

	Pronoun	My Sentence
1)		
2)		
3)		
4)		
5)		
6)		
7)		
8)		
9)		
10)		

SPELLING VERBS

Name _____ Date _____

Directions: If the verb tense is spelled correctly, color the star yellow. If it is not spelled correctly, color the star orange.

study

hurrys

plans

studyd

hurried

slams

slamed

stoped

stopps

crys

cried

tugged

tugs

sippes

dryed

worryed

119

OBJECT PRONOUNS

Object pronouns are *me, you, him, her, it, us,* and *them*.

You know now that some pronouns replace nouns as the subjects of sentences. Other pronouns replace nouns used as direct objects.

Remember that a direct object follows an action verb and receives the verb's action.

In the first sentence of each of the following pairs, the direct object is italicized. In the second sentence of each pair, the object has been replaced with an object pronoun.

Our teacher told *the class* about the field trip.

Our teacher told *us* about the field trip.

My mother bought some *pencils and pens*.

My mother bought *them*.

Use the following chart to identify singular and plural object pronouns.

OBJECT PRONOUNS		
Singular	**Plural**	**Purpose**
me	us	talking about yourself
you	you	talking to someone else
him, her, it	them	talking about another person or thing or other people or things

PRACTICE EXERCISE 9.1

Directions: Underline the object pronoun in each sentence.
Example: Sam told <u>us</u> about life on the ranch.

1. Nick read them after dinner.

2. The girl held it tightly.

3. The teacher placed them on the table.

4. We purchased them during the sale.

5. You should use it carefully.

PRACTICE EXERCISE 9.2

Directions: Replace each underlined object with an object pronoun.
Example: Ramona carried <u>the pan</u> carefully across the kitchen. <u>it</u>

1. The audience watched <u>the performer</u> walk across the high wire. _____

2. Henry will share <u>the plans</u> after practice. _____

3. The police officer warned <u>my brother and his friends</u> about speeding.

   _____

4. The bus will pick <u>Lisa</u> up in one hour. _____

5. The mayor thanked <u>Bill</u> for helping with the town clean up. _____

6. You should see <u>the photographs</u>. _____

7. Maurice practices <u>his violin</u> every morning. _____

8. The ringing of the bell startled <u>Joshua and Oliver</u>. _____

POSSESSIVE PRONOUNS

A **possessive pronoun** is a pronoun that shows ownership. Just as possessive nouns show ownership, so do possessive pronouns.

In the first sentence of the following pairs, the possessive nouns are underlined. In the second sentence of of the following pairs, the possessive nouns have been replaced with a possessive pronoun, also underlined:

Tristan's report is longer than Tracy's report.

His report is longer than her report.

Both reports are shorter than Jeanine's.

Both reports are shorter than hers.

Some possessive pronouns are used before a noun.

Example: That is *her* room.

Other possessive pronouns are used alone.

Example: That room is *hers*.

Use the following chart to see which pronouns are used before nouns or alone.

POSSESSIVE PRONOUNS	
Used Before a Noun	**Used Alone**
my, your, his, her	mine, yours, his, hers
its, our, their	ours, theirs

Notice that the possessive pronoun *his* can be used both ways.

PRACTICE EXERCISE 10.1

Directions: Underline the possessive pronoun in each sentence.
Example: <u>My</u> brother is washing the dishes.

1. Has Danielle seen her aunt lately?

2. Yours was the best grade in the class.

3. That last candy bar is mine.

4. Paul borrowed her backpack without asking.

5. The jacket is missing a button from its collar.

PRACTICE EXERCISE 10.2

Directions: Circle the pronoun in parentheses that correctly completes each sentence.
Example: Rob and Dan want to clean (their, theirs) lockers.

1. Justine helped (her, hers) sister bathe the dog.

2. We think the best story is (our, ours).

3. Please bring (your, yours) pencil.

4. Which books are (their, theirs)?

5. (My, Mine) is on the bookshelf.

6. Cleaning the kitchen was (her, hers) job.

7. The board games are (your, yours).

8. Where is (my, mine) phone?

CONTRACTIONS

You already know that the pronouns *I, you, he, she, it, we*, and *they* are used as subjects in sentences. These subject pronouns can be combined with the verbs *am, is, are, has, have, had, will*, and *would*. The combined, shortened forms of these words are called **contractions**.

In a contraction, an apostrophe (') shows where a letter or letters have been left out. For example, the contraction *I'm* means "I am." The apostrophe takes the place of the letter *a* in the word *am*.

Other contractions use pronouns, too.

CONTRACTIONS	
Pronoun + Verb	**= Contraction**
pronoun + *am*	= I'm
pronoun + *are*	= you're, we're, they're
pronoun + *is* or *has*	= he's, she's, it's
pronoun + *have*	= I've, you've, we've, they've
pronoun + *had* or *would*	= I'd, you'd, he'd, she'd, we'd, they'd
pronoun + *will*	= I'll, you'll, he'll, she'll, we'll, they'll

PRACTICE EXERCISE 11.1

Directions: Circle the contraction in each sentence.
Example: (I'm) going camping tomorrow.

1. It's going to be a beautiful day.

2. The mountains look white because they're covered with snow.

3. We're planning a trip to the beach.

4. My parents said they'll take us to a concert.

5. I'd like to visit the museum.

PRACTICE EXERCISE 11.2

Directions: Write the contraction for each pair of words.
Example: I will I'll

1. you have _____

2. I would _____

3. she had _____

4. you will _____

5. I have _____

6. she is _____

7. they are _____

8. we will _____

9. it is _____

10. you would _____

HOMOPHONES

Homophones are words that sound alike but have different meanings and spellings.

For example, words like *I* and *eye* or *night* and *knight* are homophones. They sound alike, but they have different meanings and spellings.

Some possessive pronouns are often confused with pronoun contractions, such as *their* and *they're*, *your* and *you're*, and *its* and *it's*.

Make sure you correctly spell each homophone when writing. This chart can help you remember the correct meaning of each word.

HOMOPHONES	
Possessive Pronoun	**Pronoun Contraction**
their (belonging to them)	*they're* (they are)
your (belonging to you)	*you're* (you are)
its (belonging to it)	*it's* (it is)

See the following examples of how to use these homophones correctly:

They're watching their movie. (Multiple people are watching a movie that belongs to them.)

You're working on your homework. (You are working on a homework assignment that belongs to you.)

It's so funny when the dog chases its tail. (It is so funny when the dog chases the tail that belongs to him.)

PRACTICE EXERCISE 12.1

Directions: Underline the homophones in each sentence.
Example: They're going to their house.

1. Tell me when you're ready for your assignment.

2. Do you know when they're eating their cake?

3. It's surprising that the dog hasn't found its toy.

4. They're wondering where their basketball is.

5. You're the last people to taste your cake.

PRACTICE EXERCISE 12.2

Directions: Circle the correct homophone in parentheses to complete each sentence.
Example: What is (your, you're) answer to the question?

1. Listen to (your, you're) parents.

2. Be sure to ask where (they're, their) going tonight.

3. (It's, Its) almost time for the game to start.

4. Do you know when (your, you're) leaving?

5. Let's try some of (they're, their) pie.

6. The car lost some air in one of (it's, its) tires.

7. (Your, You're) the first person in line.

8. I'm not sure if (they're, their) the winners of the game.

PREDICATE ADJECTIVES

An adjective that follows a linking verb describes the subject of the sentence.

Remember that many adjectives come before the nouns that they describe.

Example: The *famous* baker made a cake.

Adjectives can also follow a linking verb and describe the subject of the sentence.

Examples:

The baker is *famous*.

His cakes are *beautiful*.

They tasted *delicious*.

The italicized adjectives *famous, beautiful*, and *delicious* are predicate adjectives. A **predicate adjective** describes the subject of the sentence. The subject can be a noun like *baker* or *cakes* or a pronoun like *they*.

Remember that linking verbs include the words *am, is, are, was, were, be, been, seem, look, feel, taste*, and *smell*.

PRACTICE EXERCISE 13.1

Directions: Underline the predicate adjective.
Example: The baseball player was <u>successful</u> at batting.

1. The watermelon was very sweet.

2. Olivia seemed sorry about her actions.

3. My hair is messy today.

4. The new store is ready for customers.

5. The amusement park is popular with children and adults.

PRACTICE EXERCISE 13.2

Directions: Underline the predicate adjective once and the noun it describes twice.
Example: The <u>woman</u> felt <u>excited</u> after the race.

1. Joshua's parents were happy with his report card.

2. The house was decorated for the holidays.

3. The veterinarian was patient with the scared puppy.

4. Strawberries taste delicious.

5. The lake was frozen during the winter.

6. My old tablet is broken.

7. Her collection of toys is very large.

8. The roses are beautiful.

USING *MORE* OR *MOST* WITH ADJECTIVES

The words *more* and *most* are often used with adjectives that have two or more syllables.

Remember that many one-syllable adjectives end in *-er* when they compare two things and in *-est* when they compare three or more things.

Examples:

Devon is *faster* than Jacob.

Devon is the *fastest* runner on the team.

When adjectives have two or more syllables, they often use *more* and *most* to make comparisons.

More is used with an adjective to compare two people, places, or things.

Examples:

This movie is *more interesting* than the one we watched last night.

Liam's football injury is *more serious* than Aaron's injury.

Most is used with an adjective to compare three or more persons, places, or things.

Examples:

I think that Alicia is the *most polite* student in the school.

Today's game is the *most important* game of the season.

The following chart lists some examples of **comparative adjectives** using *more* and *most*.

USING *MORE* AND *MOST* WITH ADJECTIVES		
Adjective	Comparing Two Nouns	Comparing Three or More Nouns
colorful	more colorful	most colorful
curious	more curious	most curious
dependable	more dependable	most dependable
beautiful	more beautiful	most beautiful
difficult	more difficult	most difficult

PRACTICE EXERCISE 14.1

Directions: Write the correct form of the adjective in parentheses to complete each sentence.

Example: Nancy was the (impatient) person waiting in line.

most impatient

1. A gentle breeze is (pleasant) than a strong wind. _____

2. My dog is (small) than your dog. _____

3. This is the (fascinating) book I've ever read. _____

4. The story we read today is (strange) than the one we read yesterday.

   _____

5. February is the (short) month of the year. _____

PRACTICE EXERCISE 14.2

Directions: Complete the table to list the correct forms of all the comparative adjectives. The first row is filled in as an example.

USING *MORE* AND *MOST* WITH ADJECTIVES		
Adjective	**Comparing Two Nouns**	**Comparing Three or More Nouns**
comfortable	more comfortable	most comfortable
low		
dependable		
careful		
hard		
nice		
helpful		
high		
awkward		
cheerful		

ADJECTIVES WITH *MORE* AND *MOST*

Name _____ Date _____

Directions: If the comparative and superlative form for each adjective is written correctly, color the sticky note yellow. If it is not correct, color the sticky note blue.

helpful	bright	clumsy	glamorous
helpfuler helpfulest	more bright most bright	clumsier clumsiest	more glamorous most glamorous

thoughtless	fancy	sweet	pleasant
more thoughtless most thoughtless	fancier fanciest	more sweeter most sweetest	pleasanter pleasantest

cheerful	calm	slow	good
cheerfuler cheerfulest	calmer calmest	slower slowest	gooder goodest

important	anxious	large	determined
more important most important	anxiouser anxiousest	larger largest	more determined most determined

COMPARATIVE ADVERBS

A **comparative adverb** is a form of adverb that can compare actions.

Like adjectives, adverbs can describe by making comparisons. The -*er* form of an adverb is used to compare two actions. The -*est* form of an adverb is used to compare three or more actions.

Examples:

Louisa wakes up *early*.

Louisa wakes up *earlier* than Kayla.

Louisa wakes up the *earliest* of all.

Most adverbs with two or more syllables use *more* and *most* to compare.

Examples:

Lucas runs *quickly*.

Lucas runs *more quickly* than James.

Lucas runs the *most quickly* of all the runners.

I can see *clearly*.

I can see *more clearly* than my mother.

I can see the *most clearly* of anyone in my family.

Be careful not to use *more* or *most* with the -*er* or -*est* form of an adverb.

Incorrect: Ava walks *more faster* than Sarah.

Correct: Ava walks *faster* than Sarah.

Incorrect: That mountain is the *most highest* one in the range.

Correct: That mountain is the *highest* one in the range.

PRACTICE EXERCISE 15.1

Directions: Write the correct form of the adverb in parentheses to complete each sentence.
Example: Our yard turns green (soon) than my uncle's yard. <u>sooner</u>

1. The musicians arrived the (early) of all the performers. _____

2. She finished the test (easily) than her friend. _____

3. My teacher speaks (softly) than all the other teachers. _____

4. Flowers grow (fast) on this side of the mountain. _____

5. Lyle listens to the teacher (often) than Reanna. _____

PRACTICE EXERCISE 15.2

Directions: Complete the table to list the correct forms of all the comparative adverbs. The first row is filled in as an example.

COMPARATIVE ADVERBS		
Adverb	**Comparing Two Actions**	**Comparing Three or More Actions**
easily	more easily	most easily
high		
smoothly		
neatly		
late		
loud		

ADJECTIVE OR ADVERB?

Adjectives describe nouns and pronouns, while **adverbs** describe verbs, adjectives, and other adverbs.

In the following sentences, the italicized adjectives describe a noun and a pronoun.

1. My teacher is very *patient*.
2. She is *helpful*.

In sentence 1, the adjective *patient* describes the noun *teacher*.

In sentence 2, the adjective *helpful* describes the pronoun *she*.

In the following sentences, the italicized adverbs describe a verb, an adjective, and an adverb.

1. Ricardo eats the pizza *hungrily*.
2. Kevin is *unusually* clever.
3. Keisha learns *very* quickly.

In sentence 1, the adverb *hungrily* describes the verb *eats*.

In sentence 2, the adverb *unusually* describes the adjective *clever*.

In sentence 3, the adverb *very* describes the adverb *quickly*.

PRACTICE EXERCISE 16.1

Directions: Circle the word that correctly completes each sentence.
Example: Her teacher is (extreme, ⟨extremely⟩) patient.

1. I have never seen a (real, really) alligator.

2. My cat is often (playful, playfully).

3. She (usual, usually) rips up the newspaper for recycling.

4. Chocolate chips are (common, commonly) used in cookies.

5. He is very (happy, happily).

PRACTICE EXERCISE 16.2

Directions: Underline the word that correctly completes each sentence.
Example: Summer vacation passed very (quick, quickly) this year.

1. I could see the turtles in the (clear, clearly) water.

2. Teresa has a (bad, badly) cold.

3. That wool sweater is very (warm, warmly).

4. She is (unusual, unusually) quiet today.

5. It is a (strange, strangely) story.

6. All the lights went out (sudden, suddenly)

7. She played the music (loud, loudly).

8. The cashier was (rude, rudely) to the customers.

CORRELATIVE CONJUNCTIONS

Correlative conjunctions are special coordinating conjunctions. They use pairs of words to connect other words or phrases.

Common correlative conjunctions include *either/or, neither/nor, not only/but also, both/and, whether/or, no sooner/than*, and *if/then*.

The correlative conjunctions are italicized in the following sentences:

It will snow *either* today *or* tomorrow.

Neither my mother *nor* my father can attend the concert.

I'm not sure *whether* she has read that book *or* not.

Not only has Daniel won the contest, *but also* he has won the grand prize.

No sooner had she left the office *than* it began to rain.

PRACTICE EXERCISE 17.1

Directions: Underline the correlative conjunctions in each sentence.
Example: I don't know <u>whether</u> I want to bake cookies <u>or</u> a cake.

1. I'm not sure whether the project is due today or tomorrow.

2. We will go to the amusement park either this week or next week.

3. You should not only listen to the teacher, but also do your homework.

4. Neither my sister nor my brother know how to play the piano.

5. Both my aunt and uncle came to the party.

PRACTICE EXERCISE 17.2

Directions: Complete each coordinating conjunction pair by writing one of the following words on the lines: *or, nor, but also, and, than,* or *then.*
Example: If we read this book, <u>then</u> we will have read all three in the series.

1. No sooner had the dog stopped barking _____ the doorbell rang.

2. It doesn't matter whether you wear your hat _____ not.

3. She is neither unkind _____ compassionate.

4. We plan to visit both Colorado _____ Arizona on our trip.

5. If you study, _____ you will pass the test.

6. Not only did she clean her room, _____ she washed the windows.

7. Jessie was either making a diorama _____ painting a picture.

8. If the team works hard, _____ they might win the championship game.

USING COMMAS

Commas are used in sentences to show places where the reader should pause.

Use a comma to set off the name of a person spoken to.

Examples:

Is the teacher here, Ann?

Ms. Nolan, what is the answer to the question?

I'm afraid, Tristan, that your answer is incorrect.

Use a comma after *yes*, *no*, or *well* at the beginning of a sentence.

Examples:

Yes, I'll be at the meeting tonight.

No, she is not going to the birthday party.

Well, let me think for a few minutes.

Read the preceding sentences again, making sure to pause wherever there is a comma.

PRACTICE EXERCISE 18.1

Directions: Note whether the comma(s) has/have been used correctly in each sentence.
Example: Yes the, meeting has started. <u>no</u>

1. What were you expecting, Becca? _____

2. Well, she was hoping to get a text from her mom. _____

3. No, Ms. Keck she is absent today. _____

4. I'm not sure, Gabe if I'll be at the game or not. _____

5. Yes, let's go to the water park today! _____

PRACTICE EXERCISE 18.2

Directions: Place commas where they belong.
Example: Mary, did you see my new dog?

1. Well it should be a good game to watch.

2. I don't know Eric if I'll be able to watch.

3. Janice did you see the new movie yet?

4. No I haven't seen it either.

5. Are you going to the store Paul?

6. Yes you should learn to speak Spanish.

7. Well it won't be easy.

8. Kelsey will you give me your recipe for chocolate chip cookies?

HOMOPHONES

Name _____ Date _____

Directions: If the underlined homophone is correctly used, color the notepad green. If it is incorrectly used, color the notepad orange.

I <u>eight</u> three cupcakes last night.

My <u>ant</u> Becky lives in Colorado.

I will <u>write</u> my answers on the paper.

I became sick with the <u>flew</u>.

I can see the waves from <u>here</u>.

Use the color <u>red</u> to shade in the apple on the paper.

Michael <u>ate</u> a hamburger and fries for lunch.

There was an <u>ant</u> crawling on the sidewalk.

Don't <u>right</u> anything on the paper yet.

She got a shot to prevent the <u>flu</u>.

Can you <u>sea</u> the mountains in the distance?

I <u>read</u> a really interesting book.

ROLL A HOMOPHONE

Name _____ Date _____

Directions: It's time to **Roll and Write** some homophones. First, roll one die. Find the number you rolled on the chart. Then complete that action for the first word. Repeat the process and work your way through the rest of the words.

Number Rolled	Action	Number Rolled	Action
1	Write a homophone in red.	4	Write a homophone in wavy letters.
2	Write a homophone in bubble letters.	5	Write a homophone backward.
3	Write a homophone in all capitals.	6	Choose any action from 1–5.

Word	Homophone
allowed	
ate	
knight	
not	
fair	
mist	
hear	
cell	
coarse	
grate	

Word	Homophone
hair	
it's	
brake	
right	
too	
stake	
scene	
would	
tied	
see	

SUBJECT-VERB AGREEMENT

Compound subjects that are joined by the conjunction *and* use the form of a verb that is used with a plural noun.

The subject and verb in a sentence must agree.

The singular form of a verb must be used with a singular subject.

Example: Eva *paints* the walls of the room.

The plural form of a verb must be used with a plural subject.

Example: They *paint* the walls of the room.

Remember that a **compound subject** is two or more simple subjects that share the same verb.

When the parts of a compound subject are joined by the word *and*, use the plural form of a verb.

Examples:

Kathy and Eva *paint* the walls of the room.

Ryanna and Olivia *make* greeting cards.

Cakes and pies *are* delicious.

My friends and I *sell* tickets to the fair.

Heather and Joel *like* reading books.

PRACTICE EXERCISE 19.1

Directions: Circle the verb in parentheses that correctly completes each sentence.

Example: A hammer and nails (was (were)) in the toolbox.

1. Mr. Wilde and Ms. Stryke (attend, attends) the meeting today.

2. Jamie and Lisa (has, have) offices in the building.

3. Sore throats and colds (occur, occurs) often during the winter months.

4. Envelopes and stamps (is, are) available at the post office.

5. Engineers and mechanics (study, studies) many different subjects.

PRACTICE EXERCISE 19.2

Directions: Underline the verb in parentheses that correctly completes each sentence.

Example: Parrots and other birds (imitate, imitates) human voices.

1. Oranges and grapefruits (grow, grows) in Florida.

2. A chipmunk and a squirrel (live, lives) in that big tree.

3. Chocolate and strawberry (is, are) my two favorite flavors of ice cream.

4. Eggs and cheese (make, makes) a great omelet.

5. Eli and Kade (play, plays) on the playground every day.

6. Ian and Liam (spend, spends) a lot of time at the skate park.

7. Manuel and Tracy (is, are) learning about robotics.

8. Daisies and carnations (make, makes) beautiful bouquets.

WRITING COMPOUND SENTENCES

A comma is used before the conjunctions *and, but,* and *or* in compound sentences.

A **run-on sentence** is two or more sentences not separated by correct punctuation or conjunctions.

Remember that a **compound sentence** is formed from two or more simple sentences joined by a conjunction. A comma is used before the conjunction.

Example: The rain fell, and a beautiful rainbow appeared.

A run-on sentence puts sentences together incorrectly.

Example: The dog scratched at the door Eric let it in.

You can correct a run-on sentence by making two simple sentences. You can also make one compound sentence by adding a comma and a conjunction.

The dog scratched at the door. Eric let it in.

The dog scratched at the door, and Eric let it in.

PRACTICE EXERCISE 20.1

Directions: Correct each run-on sentence by writing it as a compound sentence with a comma and a conjunction.
Example: Everyone is hungry lunch is not ready yet.
Everyone is hungry, but lunch is not ready yet.

1. The audience clapped the singer came back on the stage.

   _____

2. I would love some dessert I am very full.

   _____

3. Many of my friends like scary movies I like funny ones.

   _____

4. You can ride your bike to the park you can walk.

   _____

PRACTICE EXERCISE 20.2

Directions: Add a comma before the conjunction in each compound sentence.
Example: Do you enjoy playing baseball, or do you prefer soccer?

1. Many spiders are harmless but some are poisonous.

2. The tomato soup is ready and it is delicious.

3. Laura found a fossil but I found two geodes.

4. Tim is my neighbor and he is nice.

5. Kim went to the library but she forgot her books.

COMPOUND SENTENCES

Name _____ Date _____

Directions: It's time to **Spin and Write!** Use a pencil and paper clip on the spinner to find a topic. Write a compound sentence about that topic on line 1. Then spin again and write a compound sentence on that topic on line 2. Repeat until you have written 10 compound sentences. Finally, check for correct capitalization and punctuation.

Compound sentences are formed from two simple sentences with a comma and conjunction between them.

Spinner topics: GAMES, SCHOOL, SPORTS, PETS, SUMMER

	Topic	My Sentence
1)		
2)		
3)		
4)		
5)		
6)		
7)		
8)		
9)		
10)		

CONTRACTIONS BINGO

Name _____ Date _____

Directions: Cut out the words at the top of the page. Turn them over and have someone randomly select one and read it out loud. Use a coin or crayon to mark a spot on the bingo board that matches the word being called. Once you have marked five spots in a row, you have a "bingo" and have won.

can't	don't	couldn't	won't	isn't	aren't
didn't	doesn't	hadn't	hasn't	haven't	he'd
let's	she'd	she'll	she's	what's	what've
where's	who'd	who'll	I've	he's	I'm

B	I	N	G	O
cannot	do not	could not	will not	is not
are not	did not	had not	has not	have not
he would	let us	☆ FREE	she would	she will
she is	what is	what have	where is	who would
who will	I have	he is	I am	she has

149

ANSWER KEY

ANSWER KEY

GRADE 3

PRACTICE 1.1

1. Two friends | went to the restaurant together.
2. Our science teacher | pointed to a model of a skeleton.
3. His hobby | is collecting old postage stamps.
4. Gabe's horse | pushed open the gate with its nose.
5. Mrs. Wright | bought a new pair of glasses.

PRACTICE 1.2

1. The soccer team practiced the new play for an hour.
2. The teacher wrote a quick e-mail to the parents.
3. The pitcher was filled with freshly squeezed orange juice.
4. Izzy ate a piece of chocolate cake for dessert.
5. A cactus survives with very little water.
6. A warm sweater feels so nice on a chilly day.
7. The group of deer ran into the woods.
8. A pesky mosquito keeps buzzing in my ear.

PRACTICE 2.1

1. The family was excited to be driving the new car to the beach.
2. Mr. Lee had packed sandwiches into a blue cooler.
3. The children laughed as they jumped into the sand and ran toward the ocean.
4. Ms. Lee helped set up an umbrella and beach chairs.
5. Jenny's oldest brother took his surfboard and rode into the waves.

PRACTICE 2.2

1. The team gathered before the game to make a plan.
2. The crowd cheered as the first pitch was thrown.
3. As the pitcher threw the ball, the batter waited nervously.
4. He swung his bat, and the baseball flew to the outfield.
5. At the concession stand, fans were buying popcorn and peanuts.
6. The sun beat down, and the players became extremely hot.

7. The people were grateful when a soft breeze entered the stadium.

PRACTICE 3.1

1. concrete
2. abstract
3. abstract
4. concrete
5. abstract

PRACTICE 3.2

1. What is the lesson we are learning today in school?
2. The immigrants showed great courage in moving to a new country.
3. The pioneers often faced hardships and felt sorrow as they crossed the prairie.
4. Did you share your dream of success with your parents?
5. If you think your invention will help people, you should make it.
6. The pizza was baking in the oven, and my hunger grew.
7. As we drove to the beach in the car, our boredom turned into excitement.

8. How much <u>candy</u> do you think we will get at the <u>parade</u>?

PRACTICE 4.1

1. proper noun
2. common noun
3. proper noun
4. proper noun
5. common noun

PRACTICE 4.2

1. A <u>sunset</u> over <u>Lake Erie</u> is a beautiful <u>sight</u>.
2. The <u>musician</u> played <u>Sonata Number 5</u> as <u>people</u> strolled by.
3. <u>Terrence</u> and <u>Joel</u> talked as they walked down <u>Sackett Avenue</u>.
4. We had a wonderful <u>view</u> from our <u>seats</u> at the <u>Sunset Steakhouse</u>.
5. My <u>mother</u> ordered <u>steak</u>, <u>shrimp</u>, and <u>rolls</u> for her <u>meal</u>.
6. <u>Aunt Pauline</u> wanted to buy us all some <u>dessert</u> at the <u>Hawaiian Ice Shack</u>.
7. Later that <u>night</u>, the <u>family</u> went to the <u>house</u> to play <u>Monopoly</u>.
8. <u>Weston</u> planned on buying all four <u>railroads</u> and <u>Park Place</u> on the <u>board</u>.

PRACTICE 5.1

1. <u>harriet</u>, flew, week, <u>georgia</u>, the

2. <u>everglades national park</u>, alligator, sights, <u>disneyland</u>, zoo
3. <u>friday</u>, drive, <u>gulf of mexico</u>, brought, ocean
4. <u>third street</u>, family, <u>orlando</u>, <u>boston</u>, airport
5. airplane, vacation, <u>smith</u>, <u>leah</u>, <u>sequoia national park</u>

PRACTICE 5.2

1. <u>many</u> movies are made in <u>hollywood</u>.
2. <u>the jones</u> family traveled to <u>california</u> in <u>june</u>.
3. <u>they</u> visited <u>disneyland</u> and saw the <u>pacific ocean</u>.
4. <u>mary</u> and <u>jenna</u> had never been to the beach before.
5. <u>on thursday</u>, the family walked down <u>hollywood boulevard</u>.
6. <u>they</u> ate at the <u>celebrity café</u> and saw several famous people.
7. <u>on saturday</u>, they saw the <u>golden gate bridge</u> in <u>san francisco</u>.
8. <u>before</u> they came home, they visited <u>muir woods national monument</u> and saw <u>mount whitney</u>.

PRACTICE 6.1

1. paper, singular
2. playgrounds, plural
3. beanbag, singular
4. pizza, singular
5. friends, plural

PRACTICE 6.2

1. bats
2. villages
3. glasses
4. turkeys
5. flags
6. boxes
7.

PRACTICE 7.1

1. tooths: teeth
2. gooses: geese
3. childs: children
4. oxes: oxen
5. loafs: loaves

PRACTICE 7.2

1. scarves
2. thieves
3. women
4. wives
5. dice
6. feet
7. crises
8. mice
9. men
10. lice
11. quizzes
12. oxen
13. selves
14. wolves
15. geese

PRACTICE 8.1

1. car's
2. teachers'
3. children's
4. Kelly's
5. artists'

PRACTICE 8.2

1. officers'
2. men's
3. hotel's
4. neighbors'
5. coaches'
6. actors'
7. leader's
8. Mr. Rich's
9. mouse's
10. workers'

PRACTICE 9.1

1. bark, jump, howl
2. play, strum
3. bake, mix, stir
4. swim, dive, splash
5. drive, ride

PRACTICE 9.2

1. invited
2. carried
3. meowed, jumped
4. choose
5. paints
6. told
7. laughed, cried, won
8. removed

PRACTICE 10.1

1. will perform: future tense
2. answered: past tense
3. threw: past tense
4. tastes: present tense
5. will help: future tense

PRACTICE 10.2

See page 163 for answers to this practice exercise.

PRACTICE 11.1

1. saw
2. did
3. wrote
4. ate
5. gave

PRACTICE 11.2

See page 163 for answers to this practice exercise.

PRACTICE 12.1

1. I
2. you
3. she
4. We
5. us

PRACTICE 12.2

1. his
2. They
3. Her
4. She
5. him
6. us

PRACTICE 13.1

1. exciting, large
2. popular, fun, the
3. strange, a
4. few, three
5. some, colorful, an

PRACTICE 13.2

1. He lost two hats at the old ski lodge.
2. Jim lives on a busy street near several stores.
3. I chipped a front tooth when I bit into a hard apple.
4. Darrel read fifty pages of his new book.
5. We visited an amusement park so we could ride the exciting roller coasters.
6. Many wild geese flew over the icy, frozen lake.
7. My tired mother read three e-mails before she went to bed.
8. The large group of friends laughed as they watched the funny movie.

PRACTICE 14.1

1. sweet: sweeter, sweetest
2. warm: warmer, warmest
3. nice: nicer, nicest
4. funny: funnier, funniest

PRACTICE 14.2

1. warmer
2. fastest
3. narrowest
4. greener

PRACTICE 15.1

1. My father <u>mows</u> the lawn <u>often</u>.
2. The baby <u>laughed</u> <u>happily</u>.
3. <u>Tomorrow</u> we <u>will go</u> to the waterpark.
4. There <u>is</u> a library <u>nearby</u>.
5. My school is <u>getting</u> a new playground <u>soon</u>.

PRACTICE 15.2

1. often, How often?
2. carefully, How?
3. quietly, How?
4. forward, Where?
5. well, How?
6. usually, How often?
7. sometimes, How often?
8. politely, How?

PRACTICE 16.1

1. and
2. but
3. and
4. and
5. whether/or

PRACTICE 16.2

1. but
2. or
3. and
4. but
5. because
6. and
7. but
8. and

PRACTICE 17.1

1. simple
2. compound
3. compound
4. simple

PRACTICE 17.2

1. <u>Everyone is hungry</u>, but <u>lunch isn't ready yet</u>.
2. <u>I would love to have some dessert</u>, but <u>I am too full</u>.
3. <u>You can ride your bike to the pool</u>, or <u>you can walk</u>.
4. <u>Jess may do his homework now</u>, or <u>he may finish it after dinner</u>.
5. <u>The audience clapped</u>, and <u>the band came back onto the stage</u>.
6. <u>Some people have straight hair</u>, and <u>some people have curly hair</u>.
7. <u>Holly went to see her friend</u>, but <u>she was not home</u>.
8. <u>Many of my friends like funny books</u>, but <u>I like mysteries</u>.

PRACTICE 18.1

1. no
2. no
3. yes
4. no
5. yes

PRACTICE 18.2

1. Tales of a Fourth Grade Nothing
2. Because of Winn-Dixie
3. Frindle
4. Freckle Juice
5. Little House in the Big Woods
6. The Mouse and the Motorcycle
7. The Indian in the Cupboard
8. I Was a Third Grade Spy
9. How to Train Your Dragon

PRACTICE 19.1

1. no
2. no
3. yes
4. yes
5. no

PRACTICE 19.2

1. We have vanilla, cherry, and strawberry yogurt.
2. What kinds of soups, salads, and sandwiches do you have?
3. Be sure to put forks, spoons, and knives on the table.
4. We looked at the apple, lemon, and pumpkin pies.
5. Is this pie filled with pudding, apples, or peaches?
6. I'd like toast, eggs, sausage, and bacon for breakfast.

7. Jenny, Lyle, Olivia, and Paulo are going to the concert.
8. They will hear country, rock, and classical music.

PRACTICE 20.1

1. "Will you let me use your markers?" Tina asked.
2. "Of course you can use them," Susan answered.
3. Matt's father shouted, "Look at the shooting star!"
4. "I've never seen one before," Matt replied.
5. Angela asked, "What time does the movie start?"

PRACTICE 20.2

1. "Justice has a new puppy," Grace said.
2. "When did he get it?" Emma asked.
3. Grace replied, "He got it yesterday."
4. She said, "It was a gift for his birthday."
5. "Was he excited?" Emma asked.
6. Grace answered, "Yes, you should have seen the look on his face."
7. Emma exclaimed, "Oh, look! Here he comes now with the new puppy!"
8. Grace asked, "Can we pet your puppy?"

GRADE 4

PRACTICE 1.1

1. There are many weeds in the garden.
2. The canoe tipped over in the lake.
3. The two friends made some lemonade.
4. The builders have been working hard.
5. My grandfather builds furniture.

PRACTICE 1.2

1. sentence
2. sentence
3. not a sentence
4. not a sentence
5. sentence
6. not a sentence
7. not a sentence
8. sentence

PRACTICE 2.1

1. complete sentence
2. sentence fragment
3. sentence fragment
4. complete sentence
5. sentence fragment

PRACTICE 2.2

Answers will vary.

PRACTICE 3.1

1. run-on sentence
2. run-on sentence
3. complete sentence
4. run-on sentence
5. complete sentence

PRACTICE 3.2

Answers may vary.

1. Mom called the car repair shop, and a nice lady answered.
2. The boy came to our house. He thanked me for finding his dog.
3. The line was long. We had to wait for 45 minutes.
4. Class ended early, so we got extra recess time.

PRACTICE 4.1

1. His sprained <u>wrist</u> | <u>began</u> to swell.
2. A <u>cactus</u> | <u>survives</u> with very little water.
3. A warm <u>jacket</u> | <u>feels</u> nice on a cool day.
4. The <u>state</u> of California | <u>is</u> quite large.
5. The large <u>deer</u> | <u>disappeared</u> into the woods.

PRACTICE 4.2

1. The team <u>captain</u> | <u>encouraged</u> his teammates to do better.
2. My <u>sister</u> | always <u>sings</u> in the car.
3. The <u>antelope</u> | <u>ran</u> across the open field.
4. <u>Ben</u> | <u>has entered</u> the poetry contest.
5. The <u>teacher</u> | <u>prepared</u> her lessons for the week.

6. The excited child |
   screamed with delight on
   the ride.
7. The entire class | went to
   the water park at the end
   of the school year.

PRACTICE 5.1

1. Children and adults
   waited in line at the
   amusement park.
2. Caramel apples and
   popcorn were their
   favorite treats.
3. Goats, deer, and rabbits
   are my favorite animals at
   the petting zoo.
4. Runners and bikers
   competed in the race on
   Saturday.
5. Kelly and Eric wished they
   could go to the movie, too.

PRACTICE 5.2

1. I collect and sell old
   postage stamps.
2. Jenny and Tralisa painted
   and drew all afternoon.
3. Rashanna collects, paints,
   and decorates rocks.
4. The fish in the river swam
   and jumped.
5. The musicians sang and
   played instruments during
   the concert.

PRACTICE 6.1

1. not a compound sentence
2. not a compound sentence
3. compound sentence

4. compound sentence
5. not a compound sentence

PRACTICE 6.2

1. It was an exciting moment
   in the game, but it didn't
   last for long.
2. We hadn't found the
   roller coaster, but we kept
   looking.
3. It was hot outside, so she
   planned on going to the
   pool with her friends.
4. I can't wait to go to the
   zoo, and I plan on seeing
   the monkeys first.
5. The aquarium holds
   many different kinds
   of fish, and there are
   also many varieties of
   saltwater plants.

PRACTICE 7.1

1. whom
2. that
3. which
4. whose
5. who

PRACTICE 7.2

1. that
2. whom
3. who
4. which
5. who
6. which
7. whose
8. who

PRACTICE 8.1

1. why
2. where
3. when
4. where
5. why

PRACTICE 8.2

1. why
2. when
3. where
4. where
5. why
6. when
7. where
8. when

PRACTICE 9.1

1. is
2. were
3. looks
4. seems
5. is

PRACTICE 9.2

1. My aunt is a piano teacher.
2. The sky looks
   beautiful today.
3. Chocolate chip cookies
   taste wonderful.
4. The winter seems very
   long this year.
5. The sun feels warm on
   our faces.
6. Albany is the capital of
   New York.
7. We were excited to go
   canoeing.
8. Main Street is very busy.

PRACTICE 10.1

1. My father <u>is painting</u> the living room.
2. I <u>am helping</u> at the yard sale.
3. Alison <u>is cooking</u> spaghetti for dinner.
4. The group of friends <u>had picked</u> some cucumbers in the garden.
5. They <u>will eat</u> them in a salad at dinner.

PRACTICE 10.2

Some answers will vary.

1. The family <u>had or has</u> (invited) twelve people to the party.
2. The book club <u>will</u> (meet) at the library tonight.
3. The sun <u>will</u> (set) in one hour.
4. Astronomers <u>have</u> (discovered) many new stars.
5. Brian <u>is or was</u> (helping) with the talent show.
6. We <u>have</u> (earned) enough money to buy a ticket to the zoo.
7. The class <u>has</u> (chosen) to have extra recess time as a reward.
8. Shelby <u>is or was</u> (writing) her biography.

PRACTICE 11.1

1. past progressive
2. future progressive
3. present progressive
4. past progressive
5. future progressive

PRACTICE 11.2

See page 164 for answers to this practice exercise.

PRACTICE 12.1

1. condition
2. shape
3. age
4. size
5. number

PRACTICE 12.2

1. tired, condition and hot, condition
2. excited, condition
3. Mexican, origin
4. wide, size
5. twelve, number
6. wild, condition
7. delicious, opinion
8. sour, opinion

PRACTICE 13.1

1. no
2. no
3. yes
4. no

PRACTICE 13.2

Answers will vary.

PRACTICE 14.1

1. at
2. under
3. off
4. down
5. with

PRACTICE 14.2

Some answers may vary.

1. at, after, before
2. with
3. about
4. for
5. for
6. above, through, under
7. over
8. around, near

PRACTICE 15.1

1. up the ladder
2. about the event
3. at the gate
4. under the couch
5. during summer vacation

PRACTICE 15.2

1. Charles goes camping (in) the forest.
2. They ate their dinner (before) the game.
3. I studied hard (at) school.
4. The bride walked (down) the aisle.
5. Did you know they are building a museum (across) the street?

6. There was a tiny kitten sitting between the two girls.

7. We walked around the river bend.

8. The log flume ride took us through a dark tunnel.

PRACTICE 16.1
1. no
2. no
3. yes
4. yes
5. yes

PRACTICE 16.2
1. They're
2. its
3. your
4. by
5. It's
6. to
7. there
8. you're

PRACTICE 17.1
1. no
2. yes
3. yes
4. no
5. no

PRACTICE 17.2
1. Bridge to Terabithia
2. "How to Bake Cookies"
3. "Three Blind Mice"
4. Because of Winn-Dixie

5. "Mother to Son"
6. The Farmer's Almanac

PRACTICE 18.1
1. Julie replied, "No, that isn't my scarf."
2. Duane said, "I was never more surprised in my life."
3. "Will you please answer the phone?" asked James.
4. "Thank you so much," said Stephanie.
5. Keisha said, "Let's go to the park today."

PRACTICE 18.2
1. Our teacher said, "Take out your notebooks before class."
2. My mom stated, "We are having pizza for dinner."
3. "Which circus act did you like best?" asked Gabe.
4. "How did you train your dog to speak?" asked Kelsey.
5. She replied, "I used a lot of treats."
6. Ava exclaimed, "I really love ice cream!"
7. Joshua said, "Let's get ready to go to the movie."
8. Olivia shouted, "Watch out for the waves!"

PRACTICE 19.1
1. Would you like apples, or do you prefer pears?
2. I didn't feel well, but I still went to work.

3. I had to clean my bedroom, so I ran out of time to do my homework.
4. Earth has one moon, but Mars has two moons.
5. I went to the park, and I played on the swings.

PRACTICE 19.2
1. It is raining, so we will stay inside for recess.
2. I'm going to paint my room tonight, but I might not have time to finish it.
3. Anne doesn't enjoy playing the piano, but she is very good at it.
4. Manuel went to school, and he took the test.
5. Liam wanted to go to an Italian restaurant, or he wanted to eat at home.
6. Jerry's birthday is in May, but mine is in October.
7. My mom needed some sugar, so she added it to the shopping list.

PRACTICE 20.1
Your not going to be able to see the show if you dont where you're glasses.

You're not going to be able to see the show if you don't wear your glasses.

PRACTICE 20.2

<u>many</u> people like to have pets as ~~they're~~ companions. Having a pet, though, is not always ~~easie~~. You have to ~~tack~~ good care of ~~you're~~ pet and make sure that it has ~~plentie~~ of food and ~~watur~~. you also have to take it outside for a walk ~~everie~~ day. ~~Haveing~~ a pet is a big ~~responsibilities~~.

Many people like to have pets as their companions. Having a pet, though, is not always easy. You have to take good care of your pet and make sure that it has plenty of food and water. You also have to take it outside for a walk every day. Having a pet is a big responsibility.

GRADE 5

PRACTICE 1.1

1. We went to the <u>twins'</u> birthday party.
2. These <u>knives' blades</u> need to be sharpened.
3. My <u>dress's sleeve</u> is torn.
4. The <u>players' uniforms</u> are blue and white.
5. <u>John's bicycle</u> has a flat tire.

PRACTICE 1.2

1. leader's
2. coach's
3. men's
4. coaches'

5. carpenters'
6. balloon's
7. faces'
8. friend's

PRACTICE 2.1

1. (has, have, had) chosen
2. (has, have, had) found
3. (has, have, had) sung
4. (has, have, had) broken
5. (has, have, had) thought

PRACTICE 2.2

See page 165 for answers to this practice exercise.

PRACTICE 3.1

1. A thermometer <u>measures</u> the temperature.
2. The kitten <u>chased its tail</u> all morning.
3. Liselle <u>invited</u> the teacher to the meeting.
4. I <u>finished</u> my homework as quickly as possible.
5. Edward <u>changed</u> the tire on the truck.

PRACTICE 3.2

1. The weatherman <u>predicted</u> a large <u>snowstorm</u>.
2. The scientists <u>studied</u> the <u>habits</u> of wolves.
3. My sister <u>brought</u> eight <u>pencils</u>.

4. Ava <u>chose</u> a large <u>balloon</u> for her souvenir.
5. After the parade, Olivia <u>drank</u> some <u>hot cocoa</u>.
6. She <u>broke</u> the <u>record</u> at the race.
7. All the campers <u>brought</u> <u>lunches</u> for the hike.
8. They <u>sang</u> my favorite <u>song</u> last night!

PRACTICE 4.1

1. use
2. performs
3. needs
4. wake
5. wears

PRACTICE 4.2

1. see
2. provide
3. keeps
4. cover
5. play
6. uses
7. help
8. dives

PRACTICE 5.1

1. had been reading
2. will have watched
3. has been practicing
4. will have gone
5. has been

PRACTICE 5.2

1. future perfect
2. past perfect
3. past perfect

4. future perfect
5. present perfect
6. present perfect
7. past perfect

PRACTICE 6.1

1. can
2. sit
3. May
4. may
5. set

PRACTICE 6.2

1. sit
2. may
3. May
4. sit
5. may
6. can
7. set
8. set

PRACTICE 7.1

1. no
2. yes
3. no
4. yes
5. no

PRACTICE 7.2

1. worried
2. carried
3. sipped
4. supplied
5. tanned
6. tugged
7. pried
8. slammed

PRACTICE 8.1

1. He
2. we
3. It
4. You
5. I

PRACTICE 8.2

1. He
2. They
3. She
4. It
5. It
6. She
7. He
8. They

PRACTICE 9.1

1. them
2. it
3. them
4. them
5. it

PRACTICE 9.2

1. him or her
2. them
3. them
4. her
5. him
6. them
7. it
8. them

PRACTICE 10.1

1. her
2. Yours
3. mine

4. her
5. its

PRACTICE 10.2

1. her
2. ours
3. your
4. theirs
5. Mine
6. her
7. yours
8. my

PRACTICE 11.1

1. It's
2. they're
3. We're
4. they'll
5. I'd

PRACTICE 11.2

1. you've
2. I'd
3. she'd
4. you'll
5. I've
6. she's
7. they're
8. we'll
9. it's
10. you'd

PRACTICE 12.1

1. you're, your
2. they're, their
3. It's, its
4. They're, their
5. You're, your

PRACTICE 12.2

1. your
2. they're
3. It's
4. you're
5. their
6. its
7. You're
8. they're

PRACTICE 13.1

1. sweet
2. sorry
3. messy
4. ready
5. popular

PRACTICE 13.2

1. Joshua's <u>parents</u> were <u>happy</u> with his report card.
2. The <u>house</u> was <u>decorated</u> for the holidays.
3. The <u>veterinarian</u> was <u>patient</u> with the scared puppy.
4. <u>Strawberries</u> taste <u>delicious</u>.
5. The <u>lake</u> was <u>frozen</u> during the winter.
6. My old <u>tablet</u> is <u>broken</u>.
7. Her <u>collection</u> of toys is very <u>large</u>.
8. The <u>roses</u> are <u>beautiful</u>.

PRACTICE 14.1

1. more pleasant
2. smaller
3. most fascinating
4. stranger
5. shortest

PRACTICE 14.2

See page 166 for answers to this practice exercise.

PRACTICE 15.1

1. earliest
2. more easily
3. more softly
4. faster
5. more often

PRACTICE 15.2

See page 166 for answers to this practice exercise.

PRACTICE 16.1

1. real
2. playful
3. usually
4. commonly
5. happy

PRACTICE 16.2

1. clear
2. bad
3. warm
4. unusually
5. strange
6. suddenly
7. loudly
8. rude

PRACTICE 17.1

1. whether, or
2. either, or
3. not only, but also
4. neither, nor
5. both, and

PRACTICE 17.2

1. than
2. or
3. nor
4. and
5. then
6. but also
7. or
8. then

PRACTICE 18.1

1. yes
2. yes
3. no
4. no
5. yes

PRACTICE 18.2

1. Well, it should be a good game to watch.
2. I don't know, Eric, if I'll be able to watch.
3. Janice, did you see the new movie yet?
4. No, I haven't seen it either.
5. Are you going to the store, Paul?
6. Yes, you should learn to speak Spanish.
7. Well, it won't be easy.
8. Kelsey, will you give me your recipe for chocolate chip cookies?

PRACTICE 19.1

1. attend
2. have
3. occur
4. are
5. study

PRACTICE 19.2

1. grow
2. live
3. are
4. make
5. play
6. spend
7. are
8. make

PRACTICE 20.1

1. The audience clapped, and the singer came back on the stage.
2. I would love some dessert, but I am very full.
3. Many of my friends like scary movies, but I like funny ones.
4. You can ride your bike to the park, or you can walk.

PRACTICE 20.2

1. Many spiders are harmless, but some are poisonous.
2. The tomato soup is ready, and it is delicious.
3. Laura found a fossil, but I found two geodes.
4. Tim is my neighbor, and he is nice.
5. Kim went to the library, but she forgot her books.

PART ONE

PRACTICE 10.2

VERB TENSE		
Past Tense	**Present Tense**	**Future Tense**
asked	ask	will ask
used	use	will use
needed	need	will need
practiced	practice	will practice
slammed	slam	will slam
typed	type	will type
arrived	arrive	will arrive

PRACTICE 11.2

PAST TENSE OF IRREGULAR VERBS	
Present Tense	**Past Tense**
bring	brought
think	thought
swim	swam
freeze	froze
ride	rode
fall	fell
write	wrote
go	went

PART TWO

PRACTICE 11.2

Some answers will vary.

PROGRESSIVE VERB TENSE		
Past Progressive	**Present Progressive**	**Future Progressive**
subject + *was/were* + *-ing* verb	subject + *am/is/are* + *-ing* verb	subject + *will be* + *-ing* verb
was thinking	am thinking	will be thinking
were washing	are washing	will be washing
was/were enjoying	am/is/are enjoying	will be enjoying
were spending	are spending	will be spending
was looking	am/is looking	will be looking
was wishing	is wishing	will be wishing
was/were painting	am/is/are painting	will be painting

PART THREE

PRACTICE 2.2

Present	Past	Past Participle
bring	brought	(has, have, had) brought
break	broke	(has, have, had) broken
drink	drank	(has, have, had) drunk
sing	sang	(has, have, had) sung
choose	chose	(has, have, had) chosen
catch	caught	(has, have, had) caught
say	said	(has, have, had) said

PRACTICE 14.2

USING *MORE* AND *MOST* WITH ADJECTIVES		
Adjective	**Comparing Two Nouns**	**Comparing Three or More Nouns**
low	lower	lowest
dependable	more dependable	most dependable
careful	more careful	most careful
hard	harder	hardest
nice	nicer	nicest
helpful	more helpful	most helpful
high	higher	highest
awkward	more awkward	most awkward
cheerful	more cheerful	most cheerful

PRACTICE 15.2

COMPARATIVE ADVERBS		
Adverbs	**Comparing Two Actions**	**Comparing Three or More Actions**
high	higher	highest
smoothly	more smoothly	most smoothly
neatly	more neatly	most neatly
late	later	latest
loud	louder	loudest

WHAT IS A NOUN?

Name _____ Date _____

Directions: Color all the gumballs in each row that are nouns.

Row 1 (noun): zipper · travel · listen · Main Street · planet · pretty · Texas

Row 2 (noun): curious · Harry Potter · shout · joy · First Central Bank · funny · giraffe

Row 3 (noun): cousin · bridge · swim · famous · Dr. Mix · catcher · bright

Row 4 (noun): office · carry · Disney World · sunlight · Leah · over · jealous

Row 5 (noun): broken · books · Emma · quick · peace · Europe · trail

COMMON NOUNS

Name _____ Date _____

Directions: It's time to **Roll and Mark** the common nouns. First, roll one die. Find the number you rolled on the chart. Then complete that action for all the common nouns in the first sentence. Repeat the process and work your way through the rest of the sentences.

Number Rolled	Action	Number Rolled	Action
1	Circle all common nouns.	4	Underline the common nouns with a wavy line.
2	Underline all common nouns.	5	Draw a box around the common nouns.
3	Highlight all common nouns.	6	Choose any action from 1–5.

	Number Rolled	Sentences All common nouns are underlined.
1)		The tiny kitten shivered as it say by the open window.
2)		The students painted posters to hang on the wall in the hallway.
3)		The two friends put their backpacks and coats in their lockers.
4)		The traveler carried a suitcase through Denver Airport.
5)		The commercial compares two brands of oatmeal.
6)		The family planted corn, beans, tomatoes, and lettuce in the garden.
7)		The runners laced up their sneakers and stretched their legs.
8)		His sister finished the puzzle and decided to bake some cookies.
9)		The parade will start at noon on the street in front of City Hall.
10)		George did not want to do his homework, so he read a book instead.

ABSTRACT NOUNS

Name _____ Date _____

Directions: Find and circle or highlight each abstract noun in the word search.
Words can be found across, backward, up and down, or diagonal.

BRAVERY	SUCCESS	TRUST	ANGER
SKILL	COURAGE	DEDICATION	PEACE
MISERY	BELIEF	FRIENDSHIP	PAIN
HONESTY	LIBERTY	PROGRESS	THOUGHT
LOYALTY	KNOWLEDGE	LOVE	CULTURE

```
S  D  E  D  I  C  A  T  I  O  N  L  O  Y  B  T
M  A  U  V  S  C  E  G  A  R  U  O  C  H  R  S
L  I  P  R  O  G  R  E  S  S  S  D  F  B  A  E
I  P  S  T  G  L  K  S  A  P  S  E  R  H  V  G
B  A  M  E  R  K  N  U  I  A  E  D  I  G  E  D
E  I  I  T  R  U  O  H  F  I  C  I  G  U  R  E
R  C  S  R  S  Y  S  A  R  N  C  F  R  O  Y  L
T  U  E  O  T  D  W  T  H  O  U  G  H  T  V  W
Y  L  P  V  N  R  P  R  O  G  S  M  I  S  E  O
B  T  B  E  L  I  E  F  A  N  G  K  R  Y  B  N
E  U  I  T  A  N  G  E  R  E  R  F  I  K  R  K
L  R  S  H  O  C  A  Y  T  L  A  Y  O  L  T  H
F  E  K  Y  T  S  E  N  O  H  U  G  H  T  L  Y
```

ACTION VERBS

Name _____ Date _____

Directions: Color all the baseballs in each row that are action verbs.

action verb — teacher — listen — lake — discuss — climb — short — tennis

action verb — help — pitcher — catch — lazy — sing — read — soda

action verb — near — inspire — imagine — explore — see — door — next

action verb — goes — zipper — swims — letter — aunt — ask — couch

action verb — throw — wrist — win — travel — pretty — painful — write

VERB TENSE

Name _____ Date _____

Directions: Color each star as follows:

Past Tense = Red; Present Tense = Yellow; Future Tense = Blue

went

rang

wrote

mention

wander

warned

will find

grew

appear

will travel

will eat

choose

opened

warns

needed

will ask

sail

SUBJECTS AND PREDICATES

Name _____ Date _____

Directions: It's time to **Roll and Mark** these complete predicates. First, roll one die. Find the number you rolled on the chart. Then complete that action for the first sentence. Repeat the process and work your way through the rest of the sentences. (You can write your new sentences on a separate sheet of paper.)

Number Rolled	Action	Number Rolled	Action
1	Draw a line between the complete subject and the complete predicate.	4	Underline the complete subject with a wavy line.
2	Use a highlighter to mark the complete subject.	5	Draw a box around the complete predicate.
3	Underline the complete predicate in red.	6	Choose any action from 1–5.

	Number Rolled	Sentences A | is placed between the complete subjects and complete predicates.
1)		My grandparents | bought a new washing machine.
2)		The canyon walls | are extremely steep.
3)		The two brothers | are washing dishes in the kitchen.
4)		Jeremy | finished writing his report.
5)		An annoying fly | buzzed around her head.
6)		The weeds in the garden | were difficult to pull.
7)		That cold lemonade | tasted delicious!
8)		Treydon | sanded and painted the chair.
9)		The basketball team | won.
10)		The canoe | tipped over in the lake.

SIMPLE SUBJECTS

Name _____ Date _____

Directions: If the simple subject is correctly underlined, color the crayon green. If the simple subject is incorrectly underlined, color the crayon orange.

Two <u>friends</u> watched the football game together.

Our math teacher <u>showed</u> us how to solve the problem.

<u>His</u> hobby is making model airplanes.

The <u>giraffe</u> ate leaves from the tree.

Mr. Severe has a new <u>pair</u> of glasses.

A <u>chameleon</u> blends in with its surrounding colors.

The basketball <u>team</u> practiced the new play.

<u>My</u> mother wrote the note on a sheet of yellow paper.

The <u>glass</u> vase shattered as it fell to the floor.

Eric <u>ate</u> a brownie sundae for dessert.

The rugged <u>football</u> player made the tackle.

<u>Michael</u> is always helpful and cheerful.

The <u>deer</u> jumped over the fence.

That orange <u>racecar</u> will probably win the race.

His <u>mountain</u> bike has a flat tire.

Thirty colorful <u>balloons</u> drifted up into the sky.

RUN-ON SENTENCES

Name _____ Date _____

Directions: It's time to **Roll and Repair** these run-on sentences. First, roll one die. Find the number you rolled on the chart. Then complete that action for the first sentence. Repeat the process and work your way through the rest of the sentences. (You can write your new sentences on a separate sheet of paper.)

Number Rolled	Action	Number Rolled	Action
1	Make two complete sentences by separating the run-on.	4	Color the sentence's box red.
2	Underline a part of the run-on that could be a complete sentence by itself.	5	Draw a green line to separate the two smaller sentences.
3	Make a complete sentence by adding a word or words.	6	Choose any action from 1–5.

	Number Rolled	Run-On Sentence Answers will vary. Possible solutions are shown.
1)		The dog was running in circles, **and** it made us laugh.
2)		My friends paddled the canoe**.** It tipped over.
3)		Jenny loves funny movies**. S**he is going to see one tonight.
4)		Our aunt is going on a trip**. S**he is going to Alaska.
5)		Ava is making the sugar cookies, **and** Lisa is frosting them.
6)		They started the campfire, **and** they set up their tent.
7)		We are making candy later**. I**t will be delicious.
8)		My sister is graduating from school, **and** she is going to college.
9)		Tristan studied for the test, **and** he didn't miss one problem.
10)		They were late for dinner, **and** the food was cold.

CONITUNCTIONS

Name _____ Date _____

Directions: If the word is a coordinating conjunction, color the apple green. If it is not a coordinating conjunction, color the apple red.

for	the	an	so
by	and	with	yet
yet	around	nor	near
speak	or	tree	but

PARTS OF SPEECH BINGO

who relative pronoun	**whom** relative pronoun	**whose** relative pronoun	**which** relative pronoun	**that** relative pronoun	**am** linking verb
is linking verb	**are** linking verb	**was** linking verb	**were** linking verb	**be** linking verb	**been** linking verb
has been linking verb	**have been** linking verb	**become** linking verb	**being** linking verb	**will be** linking verb	**about** preposition
during preposition	**over** preposition	**under** preposition	**near** preposition	**with** preposition	**from** preposition
silly adjective	**sweet** adjective	**kind** adjective	**amazing** adjective	**pretty** adjective	**tall** adjective
house noun	**girl** noun	**tree** noun	**desk** noun	**pretzel** noun	**pie** noun

SPELLING VERBS

Name _____ Date _____

Directions: If the verb tense is spelled correctly, color the star yellow. If it is not spelled correctly, color the star orange.

study · hurrys · plans · studyd

hurried · slams · slamed · stoped

stopps · crys · cried · tugged

tugs · sippes · dryed · worryed

177

ADJECTIVES WITH MORE AND MOST

Name _____ Date _____

Directions: If the comparative and superlative form for each adjective is written correctly, color the sticky note yellow. If it is not correct, color the sticky note blue.

helpful	bright	clumsy	glamorous
helpfuler helpfulest	more bright most bright	clumsier clumsiest	more glamorous most glamorous

thoughtless	fancy	sweet	pleasant
more thoughtless most thoughtless	fancier fanciest	more sweeter most sweetest	pleasanter pleasantest

cheerful	calm	slow	good
cheerfuler cheerfulest	calmer calmest	slower slowest	gooder goodest

important	anxious	large	determined
more important most important	anxiouser anxiousest	larger largest	more determined most determined

HOMOPHONES

Name _____ Date _____

Directions: If the underlined homophone is correctly used, color the notepad green. If it is incorrectly used, color the notepad orange.

I <u>eight</u> three cupcakes last night.	My <u>ant</u> Becky lives in Colorado.	I will <u>write</u> my answers on the paper.
I became sick with the <u>flew</u>.	I can see the waves from <u>here</u>.	Use the color <u>red</u> to shade in the apple on the paper.
Michael <u>ate</u> a hamburger and fries for lunch.	There was an <u>ant</u> crawling on the sidewalk.	Don't <u>right</u> anything on the paper yet.
She got a shot to prevent the <u>flu</u>.	Can you <u>sea</u> the mountains in the distance?	I <u>read</u> a really interesting book.

ROLL A HOMOPHONE

Name _____ Date _____

Directions: It's time to **Roll and Write** some homophones. First, roll one die. Find the number you rolled on the chart. Then complete that action for the first word. Repeat the process and work your way through the rest of the words.

Number Rolled	Action	Number Rolled	Action
1	Write a homophone in red.	4	Write a homophone in wavy letters.
2	Write a homophone in bubble letters.	5	Write a homophone backward.
3	Write a homophone in all capitals.	6	Choose any action from 1–5.

Word	Homophone	Word	Homophone
allowed	**aloud**	hair	**hare**
ate	**eight**	it's	**its**
knight	**night**	brake	**break**
not	**knot**	right	**write**
fair	**fare**	too	**two, to**
mist	**missed**	stake	**steak**
hear	**here**	scene	**seen**
cell	**sell**	would	**wood**
coarse	**course**	tied	**tide**
grate	**great**	see	**sea**

GLOSSARY

abstract noun: a word that is an idea, quality, concept, or event

action verb: a word that shows action

adjective: a word that describes a noun or pronoun

adverb: a word that describes a verb, an adjective, or another adverb

articles: the three articles are the words *a*, *an*, and *the*

capitalize: the first word, the last word, and all-important words in the title of a book

commas: used to separate things in a list and to show places in sentences where the reader should pause

common noun: the general name of any person, place, or thing

comparative adjective: an adjective used to compare two or more things

comparative adverb: an adverb used to compare actions

complete predicate: all the words in the predicate (action) part of a sentence

complete sentence: a group of words that expresses a complete thought

complete subject: all the words in the subject part of a sentence

compound predicate: two or more predicates that share a subject

compound sentence: a sentence containing at least two independent clauses

compound subject: two or more subjects that share a predicate

concrete noun: a noun that you can touch, feel, or see

conjunction: a word that joins words, phrases, or clauses

contraction: the shortened, combined form of two words using an apostrophe

correlative conjunctions: special coordinating conjunctions that work in pairs to connect other words or phrases

direct object: the noun or pronoun that receives the action of a verb

future perfect tense: tense that shows that an action will occur before another event in the future

future progressive tense: tense that shows actions that will be happening in the future

future tense: verbs that describe an action that will happen in the future

helping verbs: verbs that help the main verb show its tense

homophones: words that sound alike but have different meanings and spellings

independent clause: a group of words containing a subject and verb that can function alone

irregular plural noun: a noun that does not become plural by adding *s* or *es*

irregular verb: a verb that does not form the past tense by adding *-ed*

linking verb: a verb that shows being rather than action

main verb: verb that shows the main action in a sentence

noun: a word naming a person, place, thing, or idea

object pronoun: a pronoun that takes the place of a noun used as a direct object

participle: a verbal word that ends in *-ed*, *-ing*, or *-en* and functions as an adjective

past participle: the verb form used with the helping verbs *has*, *had*, or *have*

past perfect tense: tense that shows that an action occurred before another event in the past

past progressive tense: tense that shows events that lasted for a period of time in the past

past tense: verbs that describe an action that has already happened

perfect verb tense: used to show a completed (or *perfected*) action

plural noun: more than one person, place, thing, or idea

plural pronoun: a pronoun that refers to more than one person, place, or thing

possessive: showing ownership

possessive noun: a noun that owns or possesses another object

possessive pronoun: a pronoun that shows that something belongs to someone or something

predicate: the part of the sentence that contains the verb and tells what the subject is or does

predicate adjective: an adjective that follows a linking verb and describes the subject of the sentence

preposition: a word that relates a noun or pronoun to another word in the sentence

prepositional phrase: includes the preposition, the object, and all the words between them

present perfect tense: tense that shows that an action occurred at an unspecified time in the past

present progressive tense: tense that shows actions that are happening right now

present tense: verbs that describe an action that is happening right now

progressive verb tense: shows an ongoing or continuing action in progress

pronoun: a word that takes the place of a noun

proper noun: a word that names a specific person, place, or thing

quotation: when you repeat the exact words that someone has spoken

quotation marks: (" ") to show the exact words someone has spoken or written

relative adverb: a word that introduces a group of words called a relative clause and that gives more information about a noun

relative clause: a dependent clause that gives additional information about a noun

relative pronoun: a word used to introduce a relative clause, which in turn describes a noun

run-on sentence: a group of words where two sentences are joined together without using correct punctuation and/or grammar

sentence fragment: a part of a sentence that grammatically cannot stand by itself as its own sentence

series: a list of three or more items in a sentence

simple predicate: the main word or words in the complete predicate

simple sentence: a sentence containing one independent clause

simple subject: the main word in the complete subject

singular noun: one person, place, thing, or idea

singular pronoun: a pronoun that refers to just one person, place, or thing

subject: the part of the sentence that identifies who or what the sentence is about

subject pronoun: a pronoun that takes the place of a noun as the subject of a sentence

tense: a form of a verb that shows the time of a verb's action

title: the specific name of a book, article, poem, show, song, or other work

verb: a word that shows an action (in the case of an action verb) or a state of being or existence (in the case of a linking verb)

ABOUT THE AUTHOR

Shelly Rees has over 23 years of experience teaching students in the upper elementary grades. She loves learning and believes in providing instruction that is hands-on, fun, and engaging. Shelly is passionate about helping other teachers by creating and providing educational resources that will reduce their stress load and deliver great academic results for their students. She and her husband, Aric, reside in rural Wyoming. She is a proud mom of four sons and enjoys camping, baking cookies, and spending time with her family.